# Advance Praise

"This book delivers a thorough and practical approach for finding success with investment real estate properties."
                    **–Dr. Nido Qubein**, President of High Point University

*"The New American Dream* is an insightful look inside the world of real estate investments. Steven shows how a normal guy can live the American dream by hard work, determination, and trial and error. By reading this book, you'll learn the action steps so that you too can live the American Dream."
        **–Heather Morton Hill**, Ranked as a Top Realtor in North Carolina and Member of the National Agent Advisory Council for EXP Realty

*"The New American Dream* is an insightful look inside the world of real estate investments. Steven makes sense of an often-complex process and demystifies strategies to help any reader make smarter investment decisions."
                    **–Don Jennings**, Market President at Select Bank

"Merriam-Webster defines *mentor* as a trusted counselor or guide who, because he is detached and disinterested, can hold up a mirror to us or a wise and faithful adviser or teacher. In this book, author Steven Andrews will serve as a wise and faithful advisor/teacher to the reader on how to develop your own real estate investment business by learning from this wise and faithful adviser. I highly recommend this book to you."
            **–Randolph James**, attorney. Designated as a Super Lawyer in business litigation and as a Top 100 Trial Lawyer by the National Trial Lawyers Association since 2014

☆ ☆ ☆

# THE NEW AMERICAN DREAM

## A SIMPLE ROADMAP TO PURCHASING INVESTMENT PROPERTIES

## STEVEN ANDREWS

With Miriam Drennan

Tasfil Publishing, LLC
Voorhees, NJ

ASIN: B0CSLZMCCF
ISBN paperback:  978-1735406664
ISBN hardcover:  978-1735406688

Library of Congress Control Number: 2024903045

*This book is dedicated to my family:*
*Mom (Angie), Dad (Grant), and brother (Billy).*

*To Mom and Dad, thank you for instilling morals and values into my life at a young age. You always taught me that once you commit to something, you have to see it through, and quitting was not an option. You both live this daily. You both have always shown me the way. To this day, I still don't know how you made it to multiple games that were happening at the same time to support both of your kids, but you did. You continue to show up, and I am so blessed to call you both Mom and Dad. You have always supported everything I have wanted to do in life. Thank you for everything you have done for me. I would not be the person I am today without your love and support. I simply want to say thank you.*

*To my brother, thank you for everything you taught me growing up. You showed me that by having a vision with a plan, things could become a reality; I have applied that to my life ever since. Thank you for always being a good big brother and supporting me.*

*Without all three of you, I would not have been successful in the real estate business. God has certainly blessed me with great parents and a great brother. I do not take that for granted.*

# Table of Contents

Introduction ........................................................................................... 1

1. First Things First ............................................................................ 5

2. Is It a Good Deal? ........................................................................19

3. Financing ......................................................................................27

4. Sweat Equity and Making Money .............................................35

5. Paperwork Matters ......................................................................43

6. Maintenance .................................................................................51

7. Prepare for the Unthinkable .....................................................61

8. Insurance, Trusts, and Protecting Your Assets ......................69

9. Get Familiar with the Locals ....................................................79

10. Continuing Education: You Don't Know It All ........................87

11. Diversify Your Investments ......................................................95

12. The Rental Process ................................................................... 103

13. When Is Enough "Enough"? ................................................... 117

Conclusion ......................................................................................... 127

Acknowledgments ............................................................................ 131

About the Author ............................................................................. 133

# Introduction

I was $75,000 in debt. My salary was just over half of that in my retail management job at a big-box store. I had a dream for a much different life...but had no idea what the next ten years would yield.

Looking back, my life wasn't much different than most twenty-five-year-olds. I come from a great, loving family of four—with wonderful parents and a brother. My parents taught and lived the values of hard work, good character, and integrity. We were your average, everyday American family, all of us working hard to have a better life. For me, that meant working ten- to twelve-hour shifts. I was single, still living at home, trying to pay off my student loans—there just wasn't enough money and time left to afford an apartment or huge vacations. The little bit of free time I had was spent hanging out with family and friends, watching sporting events, going to the beach, playing golf, and sometimes just relaxing; I was so worn out from working those shifts that sometimes sleep was all I wanted to do during my down time. It's fair to say that my work-life balance was anything but.

During this time, I thought back to a real estate course that I took my senior year at High Point University; prior to that, I'd never given much thought to the industry. Sure, I figured I'd own my own home someday, maybe even a vacation home or something if I became some sort of super successful executive, but I'd never thought much beyond that.

Turns out that one course would change everything.

Now my parents had instilled a strong work ethic in me, but that course lit a fire in me, and at twenty-five, I rekindled that flame. I really wanted to get into the real estate business and practice some of what I'd learned in that course...but I just didn't know how to break into it. I mean, I was a kid in many people's eyes—a kid who worked retail, a kid whose annual salary was about half of the total student loan debt he owed. I had confidence in myself and my abilities, but real estate was still this big unknown. The thought of me scraping together funds for a down payment for anything was almost laughable when I was carrying so much debt. And who would loan me money, anyway? Real estate investors were rich, powerful, well-connected, and old…right?

Boy, was I wrong.

And eventually, my path crossed with Joel's. He was a local investor who became my mentor, and he helped me realize that this dream of mine could come true. At the time, I thought, *Wow, if I could just own a rental property…I'd just be collecting a check each month and not have to work a twelve-hour shift for it!*

Okay, so maybe I was a bit naive on some of the finer points—there is a bit of work involved in order to avoid writing more checks than you're collecting—but my dreams were that small back then. One rental property seemed like the big time to me! I knew I could do it; I just needed someone to guide me on the right trajectory. Joel helped me see that it was possible, even with the meager resources I had at the time, but I never knew it would materialize into what it is today—hundreds of rental properties, most of them purchased without spending a dime of my own money.

I hope you're seeing yourself in what I just described, and that you're rekindling a flame that might have been close to extinguishing in your own life. Everyday Americans can invest in real estate and be successful at it. You do not have to have power and money to invest in real estate, and this book is going to give you a roadmap on how you can grow a real estate company into whatever dreams you have for it, whether that is a few rental properties or a few hundred rental properties, like I have done.

From my own experience, my college degree helped me get a job that made more money to help fund my initial real estate endeavors, but that is not a requirement to get into this business. Many successful real estate investors have a high school diploma and no further formal education.

Another big misconception is that you must have a real estate license. If you want to manage your own properties, you do not need a real estate or broker's license; if you want to manage other people's properties, then you would need a broker's license.

What you do need, however, is someone to help guide you into this business. This book provides a step-by-step process on how an average American can not only get into the real estate business but on how to scale your real estate investing to fit your dreams. The greatest blessings in life require a leap of faith, so get out of your comfort zone. I have intentionally structured the steps outlined here in the order they should be taken—from first things first to knowing when enough is enough—and yes, there is a tipping point, from satiety to unhealthy greed, and all points in between.

You'll also learn creative ways to finance your dreams, how to close certain contractual loopholes, and how to build authentic relationships with lenders, vendors, and tenants. Let this book serve as a roadmap to a successful real estate business with little to no money.

Remember, I was $75,000 in debt, working ten- to twelve-hour days and weekends, while missing quality family and friend time. In less than ten years, I applied these steps and now own hundreds of rentals. Yes, my net worth is eight figures, but more importantly, I have a quality of life that is priceless. The biggest benefit of getting into the rental business is not necessarily the money you will make but the freedom of time to spend with those you love. You cannot put a price on that.

There is no mystery to this—there is only knowledge to be had. This is very doable. I built my own business from the ground up, starting with no properties and using a credit card to purchase the first two. At the time, I did not have money myself; I grew my business from a duplex to a couple hundred properties over a relatively short period of time—about nine years—without using a single dollar of my own money. It didn't take any time before my secondary income became my primary income, which far exceeded my goals and dreams as a retail manager.

Along the way, I have helped my parents, my brother, and countless others grow their own successful real estate businesses, using the same basic blueprint you're about to learn. Don't be intimidated by any of this— be inspired, be encouraged, and be hopeful. I have been in your shoes. This book has no pretense and no space for intimidation. You'll learn which documents you'll need, how to protect yourself and your business, basic management and organization tips, how to spot a good deal, how to research properties, and so on. What is beyond the scope of this book are things like local ordinances and legal advice, as those are respective to the areas in which you are purchasing property.

I will also take you through the full rental process—how to rent your property, the key steps to finding a good tenant, and a few specifics to include in your leasing agreement. Finally, what is the tipping point that makes "enough"...well, *enough*? We'll explore what that means.

If you have read this far, I already know one thing: you are enough. You have what it takes to be successful in the rental business. Are you ready to take the first step? Then get ready to put first things first.

# Chapter 1
# First Things First

The first investment property that I bought, the one that launched my rental business, was a duplex—two three-bedroom, two-bathroom units. They were nice units, and one side was already rented. The other side needed some work, but the goal was to have both sides rented in a short amount of time, which meant I had to put some money into it in order to achieve that goal.

Going through this process, I knew very little about the rental business and did not know the ins and outs, like things to look for when buying a property, making sure I knew what repairs needed to be made on a property I was purchasing, and what those repairs would cost. I didn't know that I needed systems in place that would allow me to collect rents on time and not have to hunt down tenants who were late paying, while keeping my full-time job. Essentially, I had to learn the importance of thinking things through, to make the process of buying and renting out a property so much smoother!!

This was, as we say in the South, a "baptism by fire." I had to learn a lot in real time. I was moving at warp speed, and it seemed like every time I accomplished one thing, ten more issues would arise. There was no rest for the weary, and I was weary. Still passionate and determined, but weary just the same.

Not long after that, I met my mentor, Joel. I have to give him a lot of credit for jumping in and helping me right the ship. I only wished I'd met him *before* the purchase, but we'll get to that in a minute.

"Steven," he said. "You've got to slow down, just for a bit. Before you do anything else, I want you to read *Building Wealth*, a book by Russ Whitney." That seemed like strange advice; I had a duplex unit that needed work, and he's telling me to stop and read a book? But Joel knew the rental business, so I obliged. I'm so glad I did; it gave me the tools I actually needed.

Next, Joel explained that I needed to take the actual buying process slowly. "Put the time and effort into reading the book and doing research before buying any more properties." Sure, this slowed me down in the beginning—but it allowed me to be more successful long term.

While that first duplex purchase was successful, I now realize how much smoother and more successful it would have been—especially in terms of process—had I known this information sooner.

# What Comes First?

When my mentor told me to slow down, I remember what was going through my mind: *Why would he tell me to do that?*

He wanted me to slow down because he knew I needed to make sure I had all the information in hand instead of running wild, full-blast into a business. The rental business is hard, by virtue of being a business, and it's a hard business to be successful in. Anyone can be successful if you do the right thing, however, and the biggest takeaway from that first duplex purchase was to find the right path from the start and keep the detours to a minimum.

Joel supported this by offering guidance and explaining the mistakes that he'd made, so I wouldn't make the same ones. He encouraged me to conduct research, make sure an LLC was set up to put the properties in, and build relationships with bankers so they knew what kinds of properties I wanted to finance, with Realtors who could help me find those properties. Joel helped me find a good closing attorney, which would become priceless over the years. Finally, he made sure that I knew how to be a landlord before becoming one.

You may be thinking, That's great Steven, but I've got a lead on this property, and I can buy into it now. My buddy's going to partner with me, and it's going be great. So I don't think slowing down is going to help me here—I mean, that's great that it worked out for you, but I've got to strike while the iron is hot, or I will miss out on this.

I can promise you that if you don't slow down and create your business the right way, it will crumble. Just like building an actual house, you need a good foundation. Otherwise, you will make simple mistakes along the way that will cost you thousands down the road. I have divided the rest of this chapter into sections that explain each part that should be in place before you buy that first property.

# Know Your Business

Are you asking yourself, *When will we get to actually purchasing properties?*
Trust me, we're getting there—but this is the point I'm trying to make in
this particular chapter. There are other facets that need to be in place before
you launch an investment property business or purchase a property—so
slow down, work with a mentor, and do the legwork to have a better grasp
of the business you're about to embark upon.

Your mentor is there to advise you, inspire you, encourage you...but
they are not there to do the work for you. I would suggest you read
everything you can get your hands on about this business: read books,
articles, and blogs; listen to podcasts; attend events that help you network
and learn. You want to find out what kind of rental properties you want, and
the ones you want to invest in. Do you want middle-income rentals? High-
income rental properties? Low-income? Do you have the money for a down
payment, and if you don't, where will you get it? Where will you get your
financing? What is your credit score—excellent, good, or poor? Do you have
a good income that will support a loan until you are making enough that
your rentals pay for themselves?

Think in terms of building a house; you don't just pull up to the lot and
start building. You have to clear your land, test the soil, consider where the
utilities will connect...you have to research these things before you build.
Next, you put in your footers—find out what kind of business you want,
determine where you'll get your funding, and select a mentor. Then, you
start building the foundation, which in this case would be your business,
based on this information.

Even as you build your foundation, you can't put unrealistic
expectations on yourself to know everything there is to know in advance.
Believe me, I felt the same way. This is not something, however, that will
happen overnight. You will not always have the answers. I am ten-plus years
in this business, and I still do not have all the answers! What you want is a
great foundation—one that supports your efforts and has a network of
supporters who can help you find the right answers.

Just by reading this book, you are already where you are supposed to
be—you've hit a pause button to learn more about how to build a successful
real estate investment business. We'll take a deeper dive into each of these
and more in later chapters. For now, just know that you have some
homework to do before you start buying properties.

# Find a Mentor

So if slowing down is the first part of my duplex story, and learning more about your business is the second, don't miss the significant third part of my duplex story—finding a mentor.

I cannot stress enough the importance of finding a mentor, someone who has been there before, someone who is willing to help you sidestep simple mistakes that would cost you hundreds, if not thousands, of dollars—and sabotage your success. It will require you to leave your ego at the door and really become a student of the business called real estate. If you do that, it will open your mind up to so many new ideas and to so many great people who can help guide you. Yes, reading a book or articles is helpful—but nothing compares to that individual who is there with you in real time, in real life, giving you one-on-one guidance and feedback. Someone who truly identifies with the situations and issues that you will face. Stay open to the idea of being mentored—it will pay dividends down the road.

I am so blessed that I found Joel. The information he gave me was valuable, and I gained that knowledge early enough in my career to have a lasting impact. To this day, I still consult him regularly when I encounter something new and unexpected, or when I just need input on certain decisions.

How do you find your mentor? Obviously, you want to find someone already in the real estate investment business. I also believe that when you know, you know—you'll be able to tell that your mentor is genuine, and they're giving you the right information, not just doing it for show.

*Wait, what?* Yes, there are a lot of people on social media who like to give the impression that they have more than they actually do—most of those people actually rent those assets. Glamorous photos of jets, cars, boats, even "views" of cities and seemingly exotic locations...they rent these settings for a couple of hours, several clothing changes, and a busy photographer who can post-edit the photos to appear as though they were taken during different seasons and at different times. If you want their advice, they're more than happy to take your money to give it to you; but "fake it 'til you make it" isn't advice *worth* paying for. These are not the mentors you should pursue; find a mentor who is genuine, down to earth, not flashy—because at the end of the day, the best mentors are the types who don't do it just for the money. They do it for the freedom and the impact that makes on their families. Their advice will be worth every penny because frankly, it's priceless.

When you think you've found the right person, check your gut. Consider all their attributes and solidify that feeling in the relationship that grows into a mentorship over time. As your success grows, this person is not envious; they remain one of your biggest cheerleaders and remain a source of support.

In terms of where to find a mentor, there are many avenues. There are many coaching and consulting businesses, or you can seek out local people who have been in the real estate business for some time. Be mindful that some may not be open to the idea of serving as your mentor, due to other commitments or just a general uncomfortable feeling about the role. Thank them for their transparency, and even ask them if they know of someone who might be open to it; who wants a reluctant mentor, after all? You want a mentor who is open to mentoring you and having conversations to help guide you in this business.

Finally, there is another component of mentorships to consider. When you hire coaches, consultants, and mentors, they are paid for their guidance. Do not expect free advice. That's why it's important to check your gut and find someone who is genuinely there to help you. When you find the right one, they will add value to your bottom line.

# What About Partnerships?

Spoiler alert: if you are approached by someone who wants to partner with you in business, I would really think long and hard before joining forces with another person. It might feel good to have a partner to help you through success and failures, but I promise you, not having a partnership will be even better.

In a partnership, everyone has to agree on all decisions. The complexities of this business are enough, and in a partnership, they will compound. Yes, a partnership can work; it just takes a lot *more* work. Make sure you are getting into business with someone whose personality works well with yours, someone with whom you have common goals and whose ways of thinking complement yours. You will need to agree on the type of properties you want to purchase, and lease terms when you rent them. You want your company to be an extension of who you are—your beliefs, your morals, and so on. It is extremely difficult to partner with another person or persons.

I speak from experience on this, seeing as I share an office with my family. Even though we are each responsible for our own properties, we still have a rental business to run, and it's not always easy. Everyone has their own ideas, and sometimes we cannot agree on the steps we need to take when an issue arises. That doesn't mean one person is right or wrong, but these things are what you really need to think about before getting into a partnership with anyone.

You may be thinking, *But Steven, we have so much fun together! How could this not work?* If you're still not convinced, then ask yourself the following questions about your potential partner(s):

- When we say we're doing this "together," what does that really mean to each of us? What does that really mean for each of us?
- Should our work styles be similar, or do they need to be complementary?
- Do we tend to think the same way, share similar opinions, and have common goals?
- Do we have common morals?
- Do we share a similar work ethic?
- What will be our respective responsibilities? What will be our shared responsibilities?

My final word on partnerships is an almost-cautionary tale: I had a friend reach out to me about a joint venture he was considering. He wanted to get into the rental business with another friend, and I recommended that he not do it for the reasons we've already outlined above. I remember saying to him, "Once you enter into this business, it's not something that can just go away overnight. Really think this through."

A few months went by, and my friend reached out again. "I'm so glad you gave me that advice," he said. "He didn't have a girlfriend at the time, and now he does—and now he no longer cares about rental properties or the rental business. He doesn't have time to do it, and I would have been left doing everything!"

Plans change. Life changes. If you and your would-be partner(s) haven't discussed the what-ifs, then stay out of partnerships.

# LLCs: What They Are and Why You Need One

Before buying rental properties, I would highly recommend creating a company that will legally own your rental properties instead of having the property in your name. I recommend you put it into an LLC, which stands for "limited liability company." I wish I had known this information before buying my first property. It would have saved me time and attorney fees to rework the deed when I did form my LLC.

LLCs are meant to protect you personally. For example, if a property is in your personal name and someone falls and gets hurt on your property, they could turn and sue the property owner, which in this case would be you (because remember, the property is in your name). Whereas if the property owner is an LLC, then they can only sue the LLC. By placing ownership in your LLC, your personal assets are protected. Someone suing your LLC can only come after the assets in the LLC.

There are different types of LLCs out there—sole proprietorship, partnership, and so on—so consult with a local attorney and accountant to ensure you are setting up the right one for your circumstances. Yes, setting it up this way on the front end will be more expensive, but trust me, it is money well spent. As you are just getting into this business, you might not have a lot of money to take some of these steps, which I understand. The temptation may be to just put the property in your name and hope for the best. If it is at all possible, spend the money up front to protect yourself; it will save you thousands down the road. I have already stated that it cost me a lot of money to change the deed on that first duplex so that the LLC owned it—but that also meant paying for two different closings for this property and all the closing fees associated with it.

Make every effort to set up your LLC before you buy a property. The peace of mind that everything you are working for will not go down the drain if you are sued is priceless.

# Financing

Why would I include financing in a chapter called "First Things First"? After all, how could you possibly know how much you'll need to finance when you haven't even started looking at properties yet? Simple: plant seeds, and get those relationships growing before you actually need them.

In the rental property business, you need to use a local hometown bank. Bigger banks are not willing to loan on most things you will want to finance. Local banks, on the other hand, are in the business of enhancing the community; your properties potentially bring even more business to them, as you continue to need financing, and you're providing housing for more people to move to the area. Local banks also believe in doing business on a handshake, and they understand what it means to earn your business and trust.

(Let me detour here and say a word about credit unions. Some credit unions will not loan on residential rental property, but some will. Credit unions can be a great resource, because they also act as a local hometown bank.)

Earning business in your community also creates value. Do some research and speak with people who have been in the business longer; ask them for recommendations on local banks.

Once you have landed on one or two, the next step is a big one: start building a relationship with a banker. When I met with one of the first bankers I did business with, I was told to go in and interview the banker as much as the banker interviewed me. The banker's job is to lend money, and if they do not lend money, they will be out of a job. As a rental property owner, you need money to grow your business. So the "mutual interviewing" makes sense.

The relationship goes much further, however. The banker who does lend you money keeps his or her job, but you must do your part and make your monthly payments on time. They took a chance on you, so prove that you are a good risk. When you do this, your banker will take care of you, time and again.

These relationships are significant, as they reach beyond the professional level over time. Two of the first few bankers I did business with—Don and Rick, who each work at a different bank—have become great friends. We go to lunch, talk sports and families, and they have each financed millions of dollars' worth of loans for me. They took a risk when they took a chance on twenty-five-year-old me; most people would not have.

What prompted them to do so? I had a mentor who called the bankers and vouched for me.

Joel's vouching and that handshake before I left the bank was a turning point for me. I was already approved for the loans because my word meant something to them; of course they had to verify what I was telling them, but they trusted me enough to preapprove me.

So, before you request the first meeting with the banker, remember, first things first. Get your ducks in a row. You'll want to collect the following information to take with you:

- two years of tax returns
- financial statements
- pay stubs
- current bank statement showing that you might have a little money in a bank

Bankers are usually very conservative by nature; they are not going to fully understand that you want to grow a business, because most bankers do not own rental property. Make eye contact, and keep things friendly but professional—this is your first impression, after all. When you shake hands, ask them something you learned about them when you did your research: Are they local/native to the area? Do they have children? Be personable, but not too familiar at this point.

When the conversation eventually turns to the business side of things, be clear about what you're potentially needing to finance. Explain that you are taking steps to get into the rental business, heard they were a great banker, and that you have your documents, like your LLC paperwork, prepared and ready. This demonstrates that you are serious and have initiative. Bankers see people on a daily basis who are not prepared; showing up with your paperwork and explaining why you are having these conversations before finding a property creates instant credibility with them.

At this stage, you don't have a specific property in mind, but you should have an idea of the type of property you want to invest in, a price range, and your ability to pay the mortgage on it (including what you can offer as down payment). Be transparent about this by telling them that you haven't found a deal yet but want to complete all the steps to get preapproved before entering into a contract. That is the right way to do this business, and too often, people reverse this and put themselves in a desperate position to find financing.

Why should you not wait until you've found a specific property and signed a contract? Because the conversation shifts from "I'm interested in getting into the rental business, and heard you're a great banker" to "I signed a contract for this property. Would you do business with me?" Now you're creating a relationship from the very beginning that isn't genuine. It is based on you needing something. A banker wants to lend you money when you don't need it.

A word on down payments: if you don't have the down payment money in hand, get creative. I used a credit card for the down payment on that first duplex. Don't let a down payment stand in the way of you getting into the rental business. The bank only needs to know that you have the money for a down payment; they don't need the details on where you might be getting that money from. We'll take a deeper dive into this in Chapter 3.

I would also encourage you to form relationships with multiple bankers because one banker may not be able to lend you money when you need it. A network of bankers you trust and enjoy doing business with is optimal. Think about it: for the next fifteen to twenty years, you will have to talk to these bankers on a monthly basis. If you don't like them and they do not like you, it will be painful. More importantly, if you seek genuine relationships, these people will become your friends. That is the difference between building an authentic relationship with people in business and creating relationships based on needing something from someone.

You see, this is always bigger than the transaction itself. When everyone treats everyone with mutual respect, everyone takes care of each other. Make sure those relationships are built strong, and not just because you need something they have. Start building them before you actually need money to buy property. Eventually, you'll have a banker who wants to lend you money when you don't need it. The difference here is that they want to lend you money when you don't need it because you've proven time and again that you can make decisions, do the right thing, and be successful at it—compared to those times when you need money and you are making decisions based on the position of potential desperation.

How often do you hear about someone signing a real estate contract and the contract falling through because the buyer couldn't get financing? If you're getting into the real estate business, the last thing you need is the reputation of someone who signs a contract but can't follow through.

I would also encourage you to open a personal account at each institution you intend to do business with. You don't necessarily need to move all of your personal items to one bank, but I would recommend moving your personal items to a local bank—whether it's the first banker you meet with, or the second. Open a business checking account at any institution you intend to do business with, and put a minimum of $1,000 into it. Most banks are graded on deposits; bankers love to see money in your account and in their bank when they are doing business with you.

Finally, bankers are extremely busy. As you build your relationships with them, pay attention to the nonbusiness sorts of things: be respectful of their time, show up to appointments a few minutes early so they are not kept waiting, take your cue when it's time to leave. Respect their time, and they will respect yours in return.

# Buy the Worst House on the Block

*Now* we're on the hunt. This is the exciting part—you're ready to find your first property!

Invest in a property that makes sense based on three factors:

- what you will net every month
- what kind of property you want to buy
- what kind of shape the property is in

You want to buy the worst house on the block, not the best. The value upside is worse on the best house on the block, compared to the worst house on the block; in other words, the worst house on the block has much more potential. We're going to discuss how you'll wind up with a better deal in Chapter Four, but buying the worst house means you'll have less money tied up in it and its value will grow much quicker. This applies to all sorts of properties—a single-family home, duplex, triplex, quadplex, and even small apartment buildings.

We'll take a deeper dive into where to find these deals in Chapter Two.

# Legal Representation

Who will handle setting up your LLC? Who will handle your closing? Who will handle your lease agreements and evictions? Do you have an attorney who handles trusts? You need to get your legal representation in place, and there are a couple we haven't touched on yet.

You were preapproved for a loan and you've found a property. Now you need a great closing attorney. It is the closing attorney's job to make sure the transaction goes smoothly and that you get title insurance, there are no liens on the properties that are closing, and there are no issues with the proceeds or getting the closing funded correctly to the right parties, which is a big thing.

There are attorneys out there who cut corners, so it's important to make sure you have a good closing attorney, or it could cost you thousands down the road. For example, if you're closing on a property, you should have title insurance on the property, which covers any liens that would come out on the property down the road that maybe the attorney had missed. If they miss it and you don't have title insurance, then that cost will come out of your pocket in order to settle it. Do not buy property without title insurance.

(Side note: sometimes, there will be properties for sale that are not eligible for title insurance because of so many title issues. Move on. They're not worth buying, because of the money it could cost you down the road.)

The second type of attorney you'll need is an attorney who knows rental and eviction processes. I would suggest having one in place before you get into the rental business or, at the very least, before you sign any new tenants. You'll want to talk through the rental process with them to make sure you're doing everything the right way, whether that's going over leases, how to structure your company, how to handle tenants, or how to handle evictions. In the event that you have to evict a tenant, a good eviction attorney can help streamline that process and dismantle any potential legal hiccups.

Make sure you have the legal resources figured out and available up front. When you're first starting out, it's easy to lean on a cousin who's a divorce attorney or someone's friend who handles personal injury cases, but you need to find attorneys who handle closings and the rental process that includes evictions specifically. It could cost you thousands of dollars if you decide to use an attorney who is doing you a favor—because ultimately, they are not. There are no one-size-fits-all attorneys out there.

What you might find, however, is one law firm that covers a lot of different types of law, but the firm likely still has different attorneys who handle different types of cases and clients. For example, one of the law firms I use has an estate attorney who helps with LLCs, trusts, and estate planning. Another attorney in the same firm handles real estate closings. They also have an attorney who handles litigation, whether it's evictions or cases where a tenant sues the landlord. It's nice to have one firm that handles it all—but I still work with different attorneys within that one firm who are experts in their respective fields, depending on what I need at the time.

Think of it like this: no legitimate brain surgeon is going to offer to do knee surgery at a discounted rate just so they can do the surgery. And would you really want a brain surgeon operating on your knee, regardless?

My parents always told me that you get what you pay for, and the cheapest isn't always the best. The most expensive isn't always the best, either. Do your research. Look at their references. Ask for referrals to make sure you're getting what you want and what you need in legal representation.

# Landlord Specifics and Your Rental Process

I'm not going to get into a lot of specifics in this section, because we will cover this thoroughly in Chapter Twelve and in various portions of other chapters. Since we are talking about "first things first," however, you need to understand your rights and responsibilities as a landlord and have your rental process in place before you sign your first tenant. Ideally, you will already have a firm grasp of both before you get into the rental business, but once you've purchased a property, you must have these items in place and tailored to fit the property itself.

Being a landlord is great, but not necessarily Instagram-great. What I mean by that is it's not always glamorous, even if handled correctly. Yes, you can make good money, but the odds of you driving a Lamborghini and owning a five-million-dollar beachfront home are very slim. Stay grounded and be realistic on what kind of landlord you want to be before renting out your first property.

Some of the basics we have already mentioned, but make sure you have already done the following:

- set up an LLC
- found a mentor
- purchased rental properties in the LLC's name
- secured property and liability insurance
- developed a good application process and lease

That last bullet point is a big one. Local laws will vary, but the reasons for turning down a prospective tenant have very specific parameters, some of which you may find surprising. What will the move-in/move-out process look like? What specifics need to be added to your lease to ensure your property is protected? You always want to stay ahead and anticipate as much as possible, and your mentor and attorneys can help. Make sure all your systems are in place to cover these items, where things can run smoothly. Remember, do not cut corners to try to save time because ultimately, that will cost you even more. Put in the work up front and pay what you have to pay up front to get these systems in place correctly, and you will be much more successful on the other side.

# A Half-Step Back Will Move You Three Steps Forward

When my mentor told me to slow down and put first things first, I did not understand why, nor did I want to. I believed in my ability and wanted to charge ahead and grow a successful rental company as fast as I could.

I wish I'd met my mentor prior to buying that first duplex, but believe me, I was in a much better position when it came time to purchase the second property. I was able to "work the farm," as they say, to put time and effort into properties. This way, I could ensure they would be profitable from the very beginning; tenants are taken care of, the banks are taken care of, and meanwhile, I'm building liquid cash.

My parents told me to "always save for a rainy day because the rain will come at some point." If I did not slow down and put in that initial effort, I would not be where I am today. Instead, I would have been burned out. The properties, the company, tenants, and bankers would not have been taken care of. My credibility would have been shot.

This first chapter covered the foundational items that you'll need to have in place before buying and renting properties. No matter how much of a go-getter you may be, you will benefit by slowing down, taking a half-step back, and getting these items in order. This is not a sprint—it's a marathon.

There is truth to the old adage that people can smell desperation. Be okay with growing slow. Having these items in order puts you in a better position to negotiate. You'll not only find the deals, but you'll also secure them easier because you'll have your ducks in a row. I love to negotiate from a position of being calm and not desperate, because I have the upper hand. Most of the time, when people want to sell properties, they need to sell them fast—so they are the ones who are desperate. If you remain calm, you can get a better price; the sellers are going to see that you might not need this property, but they need to sell it. So they are willing to negotiate more.

You never want to negotiate while feeling desperate to grow a business.

If your mindset is to hurry up and grow this business so you can go to your next high school reunion and brag that you own ten rental properties and make six figures a year, then you're focused on the wrong things. On the other hand, if your mindset is *I'm going to grow this slowly and methodically so this business can sustain itself*, you are not in a desperate position.

When you slow down, you're also in a better position to find good deals. When evaluating whether a property is a good deal, you need to look at the value of the property and the value of what it will make you per month, per property for the next ten to fifteen years. Let's dive deeper into what that looks like.

# Chapter 2
# Is It a Good Deal?

My next two properties I purchased from my mentor, and it was a much smoother process. Joel wanted to downsize his real estate company to spend more time with his family, and I wanted to get into the business called real estate. These were two side-by-side single-family homes. One was a three-bedroom, one-bath, and the other was a four-bedroom, two-bath. Both were built in the 1950s, and outside had white vinyl siding; inside, most of the original fixtures remained, including light fixtures. They had some age on them, and very little had been done, besides painting. We had to work through about six layers of different paint colors to locate the walls.

This particular purchase would change my mind about what made something a good deal.

I learned that if you're looking for a good deal, you never want to buy the best house on the block. As I just mentioned in the previous chapter: the value comes from buying the worst house, and then you create value by fixing it up. By doing this, you're helping out the neighborhood by helping property values go up; if you bought the nicest one on the block, everything has been done and there is no upside to that.

These houses didn't look like a good investment unless you could see that there was so much potential. Just because they were old didn't mean that these weren't solid homes; they needed some upgrades, but there was so much value they could bring in doing so. Potential value gives you the most opportunity.

When you buy a house that's brand-new, there is really no opportunity. You're buying a finished product. Buying a house that needs a little TLC gives you the opportunity to create a lot of value by turning it into something that looks way better.

# The Payoff Is Worth the Challenge

Why invest in the worst house on the block, or real estate in general? I can only speak from my own experience.

When thinking about how I wanted to create wealth, I thought about different kinds of investments, but this was the main question in mind: *What could I invest in and get a good return before age sixty?*

With stocks, you need money to put in, and in order to make money quickly, you need to invest a lot. It's the same with money markets or bonds. Not to say that those aren't good investments, but in real estate, you don't need any of that. Think about it: real estate is the only thing on this earth that you can invest in using someone else's money. Your tenant pays the mortgage, and you make money off of the property while creating a net worth and wealth—because the property value continues to go up over time.

In addition, when you think about that top 1 percent of the world, there is always a portion who has real estate.

Real estate can yield a great return on investment when you put that into practical use. Buying the worst house on the block is a good starting point. For example, buy a house for $50,000 and once you have fixed it up, it will be valued at $125,000. That would be a great return on investment (ROI). Even with putting $10,000 to $15,000 into the property, you'll still have $50,000 to $60,000 of equity in the property. That will still be a great ROI if you ever want to sell it!

To examine this more closely, you have used someone else's money to buy the property and used someone else's money to fix up the property. Now you have $50,000–$60,000 of instant equity in the property while your tenants are making the payment for you, and you are putting profits in your pocket monthly.

Please tell me what else you can do in this world to legitimately create $60,000 of equity that goes toward your net worth in less than six months…because there is nothing.

# It's Not a Sprint—It's a Marathon

Now I know those kinds of returns sound great, and you're going to want to start sprinting and create a higher net worth for yourself when it comes to buying real estate. But remember, it's not a sprint; it's a marathon. You want to create long-term wealth and income, not just short-term gains.

Never rush into buying real estate. Reread that statement.

If you've put more money into the property than the property is worth—either by paying more in the purchase price than you should have, or through upgrades and repairs—you're officially upside down in your investment. Always do your homework so you can find great deals, because you never want to be upside down in a real estate deal. Banks hate it, and you should too; you won't make any money if you rush a deal.

Being upside down isn't a good position to be in. It creates a situation that puts a lot of unnecessary stress on you. Do your home homework up front; you will benefit from this extra effort for years to come.

How do you know if something is a good deal? Something that will ultimately give you a large ROI? As you survey a property, ask yourself the following questions:

- Is the property the worst on the block?
- How much is the property?
- How much do I already know needs to be spent on repairs?
- What are my unknowns that I need to prepare for, just in case?
- What will the property be worth once the repairs are complete?
- How much is my monthly payment, along with expenses?
- How much rent will it yield?
- How much will I net?

Just a few starter questions to think about, but remember to work with your mentor to make sure you've covered as many questions as possible.

# How to Find the Worst House on the Block

So, where are these great deals hiding? Not where I'm about to tell you to start, but trust me, there is a method to my madness.

Look at MLS first—you may have to contact a local Realtor to send you available listings, depending on your location. I only tell you to look on MLS first because you'll want to get your name out there to let people know you are looking for properties. Eighty-five to ninety percent of the properties I have purchased did not begin with an MLS search. Looking at MLS will not create a ton of value, but it will create a network of Realtors who are also in the rental business and alert them that you're interested in any off-market deals, too. That's where the deals really come from; once your name is out there, you'll get calls—sometimes weekly, sometimes monthly—but you will find better deals on an off-market platform than on MLS.

If a property is listed on MLS, sellers normally want retail value for the property, and you never want to pay retail value for an investment property. If you pay retail value for a property, then you have to secure a loan from a bank, and they make you put down 15–20 percent. You'll be maxed out in that property, and you'll never fully realize the value.

I also recommend staying local, at least for this first purchase. Start looking for investment properties on MLS, Craigslist, off-market deal websites, and through word of mouth. As you build your business, cluster properties together so that you can get to each property within a few minutes.

You can also find some great deals by calling individuals who own rental property. They may want to retire, and you could find some great deals. For example, my mentor wanted to downsize, and so I helped him do that. I got some great deals from him in the beginning of my career, which made a world of difference. At the same time, I also took some of the properties off his plate so he didn't have to manage as much and he could enjoy more family time.

When buying the worst house on the block, you can expect some nice discounts because normally, you have a very motivated seller wanting to unload the property. Most people cannot see past all the damage, so if you keep an open mind and focus on what the property could be—and be sure to run the numbers, so you are confident in what you are doing—then you can find a great buy.

There are a ton of off-market properties out there, and some companies are selling them wholesale. You can get on their email and call lists to find better deals that way.

You can also get creative and ride through neighborhoods that you want to do business in. Look for properties that are run-down...look for the worst house on the block. Look up the owner—it is public record on most local property assessors' websites—and see if they would consider selling.

# Is There a Limit to "Worst"?

Yes, there is a bigger upside when buying the worst house on the block; typically, you have less money tied up in the property and you create value by adding sweat equity. You'll have a smaller loan and a value-add to the neighborhood. Everyone's property value will go up, and you should net more profits in the end.

But what if the worst house on the block is a total dump? What if it's infested with rats, or caving in? Are there limits to buying the worst house on the block?

If the worst house on the block only has cosmetic issues, then those are the ones you need to buy. Beyond that—structural issues and the like—you need to think a little harder. If a few floor joists are rotted, then that is normally an easy fix, but if the foundation is crippling, along with rotten floor joists and a lot of cosmetic issues, then I would think twice about buying it.

Sometimes, though it is rare, some houses just need to be torn down, but most houses can be saved and brought back to life. I have done this hundreds of times. It will really come down to what the numbers say when you run them, and how much risk you want to take with bringing the house back to life.

# The Payoff of Sweat Equity

Sweat equity involves you doing the majority of the work yourself, or hiring someone to come in and help you do the work at a discounted rate. When it comes to sweat equity, you really have to pick and choose the items that you are willing to handle yourself, and not put yourself in a worse position than where you started.

Anything cosmetic—painting, new flooring, carpet, light fixtures, new cabinets, new plumbing fixtures—are potentially handled via sweat equity. I would recommend subcontracting things like rotten floor joists, foundation issues, HVAC work, and so on to certified professionals. A good rule of thumb is if you need a permit to complete the work, consider hiring a professional to handle it. To simplify that a little more: if you need a license to do it, then contract it out. If you don't need a license to do it, that's something that you can potentially do yourself.

When you think about the worst house on the block, create your pricing based on what you yourself can do, and the jobs that you need to leave to the professionals. That way, you have concrete numbers to make a determination whether or not the house would be a great investment.

Sweat equity helps save you money which, in return, helps you make more money. If you hire a subcontractor to do everything, then you are going to pay top dollar to complete the work. Things that you can do yourself—and again, I'm talking about things that will not go sideways and cost you more in the end—will help you save money, and you can put that money directly into your pocket. For example, if the house needs to be painted and you have a subcontractor to price it out at $5,000, but you and some friends can paint it for $2,000, you just made $3,000 and put that money back into your pocket. You'll have more equity in the property, which is ultimately why it's called sweat equity.

# The Numbers Have to Work

I keep referencing the numbers...running the numbers, looking at the numbers...what "numbers" am I talking about? What is the difference between an asking price and an appraisal price? What is the difference between improvement costs versus repair costs? How do you factor current rent versus future rent? What is a "good" market versus a "bad" market?

To get started, make a chart of maintenance items you are already aware of; this will give you an idea of what it will cost to keep the property maintained preventatively, but you may also be looking at making repairs and upgrades. Continue to add to this, either through research or real-life experience; these are other costs to consider prior to purchasing an investment property. Do not leave any of those numbers out, because that will drastically change your outcome.

Now look at the asking price and what you feel like you could get out of the property once all of the repairs have been made. You'll compare this number to the appraisal price. This will allow you to see if you have enough margin in the property for the bank to finance it. Take it a step further and find out what the improvement cost will be, and then estimate what the appraisal will be, post fix-up cost. That's how you'll know whether you'll be right side up in the property—before repairs and after repairs—and it is extremely important to know that.

Now, run numbers on current rent and future rent. I always evaluate rents based on what the rent will be in a down market for whatever the house could rent for in its current state, but also what the house would rent for once repairs are complete.

If you run numbers conservatively, then you will always be in a good position. It's easy for a property to make money in an up market, but it's not so easy for a property to make money in a down market.

Once you run the numbers, look at them in comparison to other evaluations. Pull other comps—comparative properties—in the neighborhood to confirm what you believe the properties are worth currently and what they would be worth after repairs are made. You'll find your comps on sites like Realtor.com or Zillow, but if you have a friend who's a licensed Realtor, they may be willing to pull them from the MLS listings. Get multiple estimates from different contractors to make sure they are in line and competitive with one another—the cheapest is not always the best, and the most expensive is not always the best, either. You would probably want to focus on someone more in the middle and make sure the property passes the "eye test."

You do not want a house to look out of place in the neighborhood, nor do you want to overspend on repairs in the neighborhood, knowing you will never get your money back. This is where the eye test comes in. For example, in a middle-class neighborhood, you wouldn't want to remodel a house to look like it belongs in a country-club area. You'll never get your money back out of that property. That would fail the eye test. Compare what products you have, or what house you have, and the repairs you're making to other homes in the neighborhood.

Finally, the numbers have to work for income. You see, it's not enough to own rental property; it needs to be an income generator. You need to make income off of your rental property on a monthly basis. Owning rental property just so you can claim you're in the rental business or holding the property long term, where you can make money off of the asset going up in value over the next fifteen to twenty years, is not enough. If you manage that property for fifteen to twenty years and do not make any money off of it, you will get tired of the property because you are not being rewarded for your hard work each month. Never buy rental property just to say you have it. You want a self-sufficient rental property that is able to float itself and put money in your pocket on a monthly basis while it appreciates.

# Don't Waste Short-Term Success

Remember the two properties I mentioned at the opening of this chapter? I tripled my investment. Let me explain to you how I bought a good deal and how it turned into a great deal.

I bought them for $45,000 apiece, which meant I had $90,000 tied up in both of them from the start, money that the bank financed. They were both the worst two houses on the block and needed cosmetic work. I provided sweat equity and got the work done on the property for pennies on the dollar—approximately $10,000 for both properties. Some of the work I was able to do myself, and some of it I had to get other people to do since I was still working a full-time job. Now I had $100,000 total tied up in both properties, and together, they were now worth about $150,000. With the properties in better shape, I could raise the rent *and* go back to the bank to refinance them, turning all my sweat equity into cash.

I went back to the bank that originated the loan and was able to get 85 percent of that $150,000 in a cash-out refinance, which put the loan around $127,000. After closing costs and appraisal fees on the refinance, I was able to put $25,000 in my pocket. Then I moved on to the next property, and continued to buy more. Over the next fifteen years, the tenants will make those payments for me and pay off the $127,000 loan. This will generate additional income for me, and the rental properties will appreciate, as long as I take care of them and keep them properly maintained. Remember, I ran the numbers in advance to make sure I could maintain them and still make a profit.

These purchases yielded great short-term success because I was able to buy them at a great price. I was able to fix them up and raise the rent, but also pull my sweat equity out and roll it into the next property.

I would also consider these great long-term successes. You never want to fully pull out a hundred percent of your equity, because you will then be upside down in your property, which would then turn into a bad deal. So by having short-term success with a property, it set me up to have long-term success. Don't waste that short-term success using the money to buy a luxury car or a boat, because those items will never make you money; in fact, they are depreciating assets. You always want to use the equity to buy other appreciating assets that will not only go up in value every year and over time, but also make you money over time.

This is how you can use someone else's money to create great wealth, and also use your tenants' rent to pay your mortgage payment on a monthly basis. There is no other business in the world that allows you to do this. Not only are you making money using someone else's money, but you are also creating wealth using someone else's money, and generating income every month while your tenants pay off your debt. It's a great business model.

# Chapter 3
# Financing

My mentor Joel and I met early in my real estate career, when I was just getting started. My father had known him for years and suggested I reach out to him; he felt Joel would be a great resource for me, as he had a wealth of knowledge to help me get started. I took his advice, and I have never, ever regretted it.

It was such a great match, because he was wanting to downsize his business and I was wanting to grow mine, and our personalities meshed together. The things he taught me back then were priceless, and nine years later, he's still teaching me.

Remember, the relationships you build in this business need to be authentic, and not just using people to get what you want from them. My relationship with Joel is just that; we initially got together and talked about business, but a bond was created over time. It's a bond of trust, and one I wouldn't violate or trade for anything.

Joel would always remind me that authentic relationships are key because that is a part of the foundation of a great business—especially when it comes to financing. He connected me with a local banker named Don, whom I use to this day. Now, the driving reason to meet Don was to get a loan to help fund the real estate business I wanted—that's true, but that was not my sole intention. I had the mindset that bankers are people who would help finance my dreams, but don't miss that first part—*bankers are people*. They have good days, bad days, life events, and interests outside of their work. That mindset—remembering that bankers are people—has paid dividends that cannot be measured.

## Building a Bridge

My parents instilled in me early on that relationships matter. They owned a landscaping business and knew their handshake was as binding as a contract. You keep your word, do what you say you're going to do. These same lessons were reinforced by Joel, who emphasized that an authentic relationship is a two-way street, not one-way.

When you approach relationships in business, yes, there is an end goal; however, to be successful, it really needs to go beyond that. Genuine relationships are not merely transactional. If they're in a tough spot, what can you do to help? When you're in a tough spot, those who are genuine will also respond, because they know you would do the same, or have done the same, for them.

So how do we build that bridge between the transactional and the personable to form an authentic relationship?

Likely, that first meeting will be strictly business, but there's no reason you can't start by asking them how their day is going. If they have been in back-to-back meetings or just hung up from an exhaustive phone call, give them a moment to catch their breath. They may tell you, "I haven't had time for lunch yet," or "My child forgot his soccer uniform, and they have an away game," or something else that gives you insight into their life or position at the bank.

That doesn't mean you have to offer to go get the child's uniform or bring them lunch...but those are small details to make note of as you get to know them better. Maybe on your next visit you can ask how their child's soccer season is going or bring them a small treat from a bakery. As you navigate your financing and discuss new loans, listen to what is going on in the banker's world: Do they take care of elderly parents? Is their spouse ill? Did your town recently experience a storm, and if so, was their house affected by it? Over time, you will gauge how to interact even better with them. Maybe an occasional phone call just to say hello and see how they're doing, or if you know they are dealing with a personal issue, let them know you're thinking about them and want to help or support them. These are things you would normally do for your friends, right? Perhaps at a deeper level, but the attributes are similar. Every interaction does not have to be about business.

# Financing Options

When it comes to actually financing your dreams, there are quite a few options. Some of them are more creative than others.

## Banker Financing

The first one is good ol' banker financing. Find a local bank, find out which banker you need to talk to, and set up a meeting. Let the bank know you're bringing all the documents we've discussed: tax returns from the last two years, financial statements, pay stubs, bank statements. This gives you immediate credibility with the lender. Be careful not to act pushy or desperate; if you do, the banker will let you know what they can do in the terms that they can approve you for—normally, 70 to 85 percent of the loan-t0-value ratio that they can loan, and you'll have to come up with a difference. Interest rates will vary, and normally, you can get a fifteen- to twenty-year note on the properties. Sometimes you can even get a twenty-five-year note (I would not recommend getting a ten-year note, because you can always pay extra on a note with a longer term, and it also gives you the flexibility to not pay as much as you would be required to pay on a ten-year note).

The bank may make you get an appraisal on the property, and if the appraisal value is enough to justify the loan amount, you'll be good to move forward. If the appraisal comes in under the loan amount, then you'll have to come up with a difference to pay for the property at closing. These types of loans are normally refinanced every five years, so keep that in mind. Property values, interest rates, et cetera, can all change in five years. And again, if the property doesn't appraise for enough at that time, then you will still have to pay the difference. That's why it is so important to avoid getting upside down in a property.

## Seller Financing

Seller financing is another great tool to help you finance your dreams. Normally, people will finance their properties when they do not want to get killed in taxes, which can happen when you get a lump sum of money through selling a property.

When you are structuring a seller-finance deal, you might pay a little bit more for the property than you would if you financed through a bank, and your interest rate may be a bit higher (though I've seen it go both ways, so expect higher and celebrate if it's lower). Usually, however, you won't have nearly as much of a down payment.

Seller financing is great because normally, you don't have to have it appraised, and you don't have to ensure the same approval process for the loan. It usually involves a conversation with a person who owns the property—the seller who is providing the financing. The conversation will be very similar to the one with the bank, but you do not typically have to supply as much in supporting documents.

The loan is usually just based on the numbers that make sense for both parties, so make sure you run the numbers. Seller financing can be the best of both worlds when it comes to both parties winning—especially the seller, who is providing the financing.

The seller is acting as the bank, and will close the properties just like you would with a bank, minus the required appraisal. You can always get an appraisal if you want to, but a simple market analysis to find comps to support the value would be good enough.

I've used seller financing in several deals, and they have worked out great because you do not have as much out-of-pocket expense, like the down payment...and I was okay if the interest rate and purchase price were just a little bit elevated, even in those cases. Normally, seller financing deals are a win-win for both parties, so keep that in mind when you're looking to structure a deal like this.

## Rent-to-Own or Lease, with an Option to Buy

You don't see a lot of people using this type of financing, and I have personally never closed properties using either of these options, but I have been on the financing side of this. I have entered into a contract using rent-to-own and a lease with an option to buy as the lien-holder of properties. These two are similar, but there are some slight differences.

With a rent-to-own property, the property owner leases out a property to the tenant (the "lessee") for a set monthly amount, part of which will be applied to principal every month. Usually, the lessee puts down a small down payment on the property, and they are required to handle all upkeep of the property. This does vary among state laws, so you will need to contact your local attorney to verify.

If they do not pay the rent, then that would be considered a default, and you would go through the legal process to get your property back. You would keep all the rent paid and the down payment—neither of that is refundable, if the deal has been structured correctly. A default is more complicated than a standard eviction, and you want to make sure you have an attorney who is willing to handle a default situation.

Lease with an option to buy is very similar to rent-to-own, but there are a few differences. I have not purchased any properties using this financing method, but I have provided financing using this structure. You agree on an asking price and sign an agreement. You'll also come up with an agreed leasing price and down payment, usually called a "fee for the option" in this scenario. For example, if you have a $100,000 property, you've agreed to that as the purchase price, and you're looking to do a lease with an option, your option fee would be $10,000, which gives you the right to buy the property at a certain date.

The seller comes up with a monthly rental amount, and then when the option date comes, the lessee has the option to buy the property, or the seller has the option to take the property back if they do not buy the property. The difference between a rent-to-own and a lease with an option to buy is that with the former, there is already an expressed intent to buy, and a portion of the rent goes toward that purchase until the property is paid off. In the latter, the property is leased, but they must agree to purchase by a certain date; the "fee for the option" guarantees that.

Both of these certainly make sense for the property owner executing this deal, but there are cases where it does not make sense for the buyer. This could be a good option if you don't have a lot of money or if you don't have good credit. Sometimes, however, you need creative ways like seller financing to help finance your dreams if a bank option is not available.

# They Need You As Much As You Need Them

We have touched on this briefly, but it's easy to forget. Yes, financing is important in the real estate business. But remember, you are interviewing the lender as much as they are interviewing you. You do not want to do business with someone you don't like. After all, you are potentially dealing with them for the next fifteen to twenty years.

Also keep in mind that the banker wants to loan you money when you don't need it. A pushy or desperate borrower doesn't go over well from the other side of the desk. Strike a balance there—you're on the begging end, so pushiness doesn't fly, but the world will not end if this particular lender doesn't want to play ball. You'll find someone else who will, so there is no need to act desperate.

Now, all four of the financing options I presented in this chapter can benefit you in many ways, but the biggest long-term benefit will be the relationships you build along the way, not only with the banker but also with anyone who helps finance your dreams. You need to establish a good relationship with each lender, and make sure you don't have the mindset to just "take the money and run." That type of relationship will get you nowhere and will quickly label you among lenders; at some point, the money will dry up.

When you build great relationships with people who finance your dreams, it can be mutually beneficial. That's why you want to come from a place of being genuine and authentic, not just from a place of needing money they can potentially supply to you. I consider each of the individuals who have financed deals through me or for me a friend. Whether I have borrowed from them or they have borrowed from me, we can look each other in the eye, go to lunch, and talk about something other than business. It's that real, and that genuine.

As you build these relationships, it is always better to have multiple avenues of financing: multiple banks and individuals. Relationships are key, but spreading the business among multiple lenders is also key. The banker has to lend money to keep their job, but it also has to be a good loan. The same rule applies with your financing—you don't want to just give one banker all your business. That way, all of your sources of funding will be happy, but you're also creating credibility and building great relationships.

Having multiple lenders is also a good idea because one banker cannot finance everything you want them to. When one says *no*, you have another one who will say *yes*. I've never had all my lenders say *no* at the same time; I've been able to get a *yes* and continue to grow my business. Keep in mind when a banker says *no*, most of the time it has nothing to do with you and more to do with the bank and their position in the current market...and with what they have currently on their books. Do not take that *no* personally, and be respectful of their decision; remember, this relationship goes far beyond what business holds and is an authentic, genuine relationship. When one says *no*, thank them for their time, be respectful, and move on to the next banker to get the deal funded.

# Deposits That Pay Dividends

We touched on this in Chapter One, but just to reiterate, bankers care also about things like deposits in their bank. Not only is a bank graded on the loans that they have provided, but they are also graded on the deposits. This is huge.

If you want a banker to lend you money, make sure you're also putting money into their bank, even if it is just a thousand dollars or so. That will show that you appreciate what they're doing for you and that you also understand how banking works.

Bankers love to be able to pull up your account and see how much money you have in their bank. This will obviously grow over time, as your bank accounts grow, and it becomes a lot easier to ask for a loan as your account grows. The banker wants to see that you have money in their bank to fund those monthly payments that you have with them; keep in mind that this practice took me years to get to, so it's perfectly okay that you're not at this point today.

So you might also be thinking, *How in the world am I going to keep all these loans straight if I'm at multiple institutions? And won't that create risk for me?* If you put certain measures in place, it will not be complicated at all, and you are actually going to have *less* risk by having accounts at multiple banks and institutions.

Think it through: if everything was at one bank and all your loans and checking accounts were there as well, then all it would take is for one bank to call all those notes, and you wouldn't be able to do anything about it. By spreading loans and deposits over multiple banks, the odds of every bank calling every note at one time are pretty slim.

I've had friends with thousands of dollars in the bank, great credit scores over 800, and great paying history, and they were right side up in every deal. The bank still called their note because it had nothing to do with them and had everything to do with the position the bank was in. My parents always told me, "Don't put all your eggs in one basket." Spread the love over multiple banks and institutions, and you will be much better off in the long run. Plus, you'll be able to grow faster because when one bank tells you *no*, you have a relationship with another bank that will say *yes*.

# Credibility and Accountability

I mentioned earlier that I still go to Don and Rick, the two bankers who helped me launch my business over a decade ago. At the time of this writing, I've closed millions of dollars with them both, and they are lenders at local banks here in my hometown...but more importantly, I call them friends. The world of banking and real estate is like a fraternity of men and women; if you take care of those who take care of you, word will spread that you're a reliable source of business.

The cool part is, when it was time to build more relationships with lenders, the new banks would call my old banks for references. This gave me even more credibility with all the new institutions I did business with, which grew not only my professional relationships but also my circle of friends—not to mention, strengthening the bond among older friends, because I honored the kind words they said about me and became just as reliable with the newer lenders. Without these relationships, I would not have the company I have today, making seven figures a year.

As you continue to build these relationships, you should be accountable for all your personal and business decisions. If you aren't accountable for your actions, then not only will these relationships fall apart and you will no longer get financing, but your business will fall apart, too. People who are willing to vouch for you are putting their own reputations on the line; make sure to hold yourself personally and professionally accountable for your actions so that people that have taken care of you will also be taken care of. Your monthly payments, financial statements, taxes, fixing up your properties and maintaining them properly, and staying respectful even when the lenders have to tell you *no* will earn you the sort of capital that money can't buy.

Taking accountability one step further, be a good steward with the money you spend to make sure that you are bringing in more money than is going out. This helps you build trust and credibility with the individuals at the institutions that help finance your dreams. Those who work at banks and who help finance deals are generally conservative people at heart, so the last thing they want to see you do is take money from the bank or your profits to go buy a luxury car or a nice boat when they would rather you put that money back into the business.

One thing that helps control these expenses is sweat equity. In the next chapter, we will dive deeper into how sweat equity can save you thousands in expenses but also help you grow and create the business of your dreams.

# Chapter 4
# Sweat Equity and Making Money

Sometimes, when you are in the moment and cash is tight, you may be tempted to make cheaper fixes instead of long-term or even permanent fixes.

Those cheaper fixes will often cost you more money. I learned this the hard way.

I'd purchased a property that needed new flooring, among other repairs, and didn't have a lot of cash on hand to fix it up. Using the cheapest flooring, I was able to turn the house quickly and get a tenant into the property faster. The flooring looked really good, actually, so I was pleased with all the outcomes.

Not even a year later, that cheap vinyl flooring tore, and I had to fix it before it got worse. This time, I used a mid-grade LVP flooring, which has held up just fine. Lesson learned.

The moral of my story: you might have a very tight budget, but there are certain repairs on which you should never cut corners. Flooring is one of them.

## Is It Ever Okay to Take a Cheaper Route?

Now that doesn't mean that every repair or upgrade has to be luxury-level and top-of-the-line. I am saying, however, don't go on the cheap, no matter how good something may seem. That first round of flooring looked great; it might have worked well for some sort of display or a theater set, but it could not withstand daily use. In a matter of months, it was tearing up, and had a tenant tripped and fallen, I would have had bigger problems than replacing the flooring.

There are some ways to save money when it comes to making repairs and renovations. For example, sometimes doing it yourself is a good idea...and sometimes it's not.

When I think about repairs that I'm willing to do myself, I would make repairs that tend to be more cosmetic—painting, sheetrock work, yard maintenance, trimming shrubs and trees, maybe even changing out a window or door if it's fairly straightforward. Things I would not do myself, and recommend you don't either, unless you have a license to do so, would include HVAC, electrical, and plumbing work, just to name a few. I would leave those to the licensed professionals. If there is any sort of structural work that needs to be one, I strongly recommend you leave that to the professionals as well. A good rule of thumb is if it requires a license, don't do it yourself.

# Handyman versus Contractor

Many times, those who are new to this business think hiring a handyman is the same as hiring a contractor. While this isn't correct, the difference between the two is actually quite simple.

A handyman is someone who has their own crew or will be doing the work themselves. A contractor is someone who will sub out the work out to different crews. So why does that matter?

You will usually get a better price using a handyman than a contractor, because that handyman either does the work or has people on payroll who will do the work; you will not have a middleman taking a cut from the price of work being done, which would keep the price from going up. Usually, the quality of work will be the same and it will save you money. So why hire a contractor, then?

With a handyman, it might take a little bit longer to get the project done because they do not sub out any of the work. They only use the crews that are on their payroll, or they do the work themselves.

A contractor will come at a higher price, but you could potentially get the work done a little faster—and sometimes, you're on a deadline. They are, essentially, the middleman between you and the subcontractor—the various crews who will do the work. The contractor will hire based on availability and price, then take a cut on top of what the crew normally charges (usually, about 20 percent).

This is a classic circumstance of money versus time. To reiterate, the quality of the work is usually the same.

The scope of the project may also factor into whether you would choose one over the other. For example, if your foundation is cracked and sinking, or you have structural issues with the property, you will need to hire a contractor; they, in turn, will hire licensed subcontractors who will not only handle the work itself but also the permits and inspections required before and after the job is completed. This is not something that a handyman could do for you.

A handyman would be used for cosmetic issues that you are not willing or able to handle yourself—painting, new flooring, installation of plumbing and lighting fixtures, and so on. Water lines, new wiring, and other things like that shouldn't be handled by a handyman—those sorts of things should be handled by those who are licensed to do that work.

Therefore, it is important that you build a roster of handymen and contractors. Both are very important to your success in real estate, because sometimes, you will need to pay a little more to get something done faster, or the work is very specific to licensed professionals. You may have your preferences, but anything can change—sudden change in health, retirement, a move, or simply availability. Make sure you always have options, and a roster will keep you from any last-minute scrambles.

When the job could be handled by either a handyman or contractor, and you have the luxury of time, then it will be worth paying a bit less for the same quality of workmanship. You will need to evaluate these situations on a case-by-case basis to determine which one makes the most sense to you.

# How to Evaluate a Bid

By now, you might be thinking, These are investment properties, not my primary residence—shouldn't I always go with the least expensive bid? Why would I put a lot of money into something I don't live in? If a handyman says he can rewire something, wouldn't that save me money?

I'm going to say at the offset that yes, these are investment properties and not your primary residence; however, they will be *somebody's* primary residence. The most expensive—be it an item or service—doesn't always yield the best quality, but I can almost assure you that the cheapest might deliver the worst.

Let me clarify that. When you are new to this business and taking bids for the items that need to be fixed and for renovations at your rental property, be very cautious about who you hire. Yes, price is one consideration, but you also need to consider the quality of their work, which means getting *and actually checking* references. Always, always get bids; this is why you keep a roster and don't just have one handyman or one contractor. I also recommend getting multiple bids per job. If one is considerably lower, be very cautious and vet them thoroughly. They may be just starting out and trying to build their business...or there may be something else going on.

As you build your roster of handymen and contractors, you'll keep the ones who did a good job. So usually, you will have already filtered out the bad guys, and as you gain more experience, you will have a better gauge when adding someone new to your roster.

Most of the time, I get multiple bids, and sometimes, they are all within reason. At this point, I have worked with everyone on my roster on a number of projects. So, if they are all within a few dollars of each other, how do I evaluate a bid?

When this happens, price is always the top consideration, but I also consider the quality and the time it would take. If I know I have a very busy few weeks ahead of me, I consider their work style—are they the type who contacts me frequently, or someone who just gets in there and gets the work done? By the same token, is this the sort of job where I *want* to be in constant contact with them, and will they honor that? Make sure your work styles align and communication frequency is agreed upon in advance; clearly define when it's acceptable for the contractor to make decisions on their own, and that they will honor that.

I don't plan it this way, but when I look at the various projects I've hired out over the years, it's fair to say that I don't go with the cheapest bid and rarely go with the most expensive. Sometimes, pricing does not correlate with a good job, but I take a look at the price compared to quality and the amount of time they request to do it. Then, I follow up with references and, when I can, actually view similar work that they have completed. Yes, every time. No matter how long I've been working with them. Why?

At the end of the day, if they cut corners and they do a subpar job, it's not going to matter what I pay. I'm going to have to pay someone else to come back out there and do the work again down the road. Remember, it may not be your primary residence—but it will be someone else's.

# How Much Will I Save?

Hopefully, your wheels are turning: What are some things I'm comfortable handling? What should I probably hire out? What are some things I could learn, over time, by taking a class or asking my mentor?

I have a lot of stories that illustrate the pros and cons of doing it yourself and hiring out projects, but in terms of making final decisions about who will do what, consider the amount of money you can save by doing it yourself...so long as you do not jeopardize the quality of work.

The more you can handle on your own—again, without compromising the quality—the more you can funnel into repairs that you need to hire out, like structural issues. Too often, people try to attempt the structural work themselves, rigging up fixes that ultimately make matters worse. I've seen it happen time and again. They are putting themselves in a position of liability, decreasing their property value by causing a bigger repair down the road, and jeopardizing the well-being of those who will live in the home. Get those sorts of things done correctly the first time—I cannot stress this enough.

Now for those things you can do yourself, you can expect some big savings, possibly up to 60 percent. The materials will cost about the same, so the real savings come from the labor costs.

You always want to spend money accurately, and not recklessly. What I mean by that is if you have three quotes to paint a house, and one is way higher than the others but the quality across the board is the same, or the referrals are all the same, you're going to get relatively the same paint job. Going with the most expensive person would be spending money recklessly.

Also keep in mind that "if it's not broke, don't fix it." For example, if you have a light fixture that is relatively new, still works, and still looks good, don't change it out just to be changing the light fixture. That would also be classified as reckless spending because you did not gain anything by changing the light fixture if there was nothing wrong with it.

The amount of money that you save by doing some of the repairs yourself, you need to either roll into more significant repairs on the current property, roll it into the next property, or roll it back into your business. Do not roll that into a brand-new car, boat, or cell phone. You want to take your hard-earned savings and continue building your business, even if you don't want any more rental properties. There will come a day when you'll need those savings. As my parents always told me, save for a rainy day...because the rain will always come. You need to be prepared for it.

I know that sometimes on social media, you see these alleged real estate professionals living a lavish lifestyle and it looks amazing, and you wish you had that—but don't believe everything you see on social media. I am in the top 1 percent of earners and net worth—not only in real estate, but in the whole country—and I do not have some of the things that you see on social media. Real estate is not as lavish as what you see on social media; what you see are the great things that real estate could potentially give you if you do all the right things and have a ton of success, but rarely do you see the challenging parts.

Don't spend recklessly, and certainly don't practice the "fake it 'til you make it" philosophy.

# Refinancing

After making the necessary repairs, you might consider refinancing the property to pull your money out, known in the industry as a "cash-out refi." This is where all that sweat equity puts money back into your pocket. It helps you scale and grow your business using the bank's money.

In terms of timing, I recommend you wait until after you've made the necessary repairs. That way, your hardworking capital that is currently tied up in one property can roll into the next real estate deal, allowing you to buy more property without having any of your own money tied up in it. By using the bank's money, you will earn more money. When you cash out, you are taking your working capital that is still within the property (maybe the amount even increased after the sweat equity that was put into the property) and pulling it out by refinancing your loan to have a bigger loan on the property; that will also put the money into your pocket, enabling you to roll that money into the next property. So this helps you grow not only your business but also your net worth, and it frees up your time, which I believe is the most important part.

I will warn you that cashing out has a tremendous lure. It's thousands of dollars, and the temptation will be there. You spotted a great deal on a boat, or your favorite airline is having a sale on international travel. Or maybe you've been eyeing a motorcycle that you've dreamed of owning since you were a child. Do. Not. Go. There.

You do not want to roll this money into a depreciating asset. By rolling that money into your next real estate investment, you're investing in an appreciating asset. I realize that this may be the first time you've ever had this much cash at one time, and you've never owned a pair of designer shoes or a sofa that wasn't secondhand. An asset that appreciates goes up in value over time, and a depreciating asset goes down in value over time. Real estate is an appreciating asset; a car, a boat, and yes, even designer shoes are depreciating assets. You never want to use your refinance money from real estate to buy a depreciating asset; that is the easy way to lose all your hard-earned money and place yourself in a position to fail in this business.

I have seen this happen far too often. Those new to real estate cash out and then buy an expensive car, and later, they can no longer afford it. If it's not repossessed, they have to sell it. They not only lose money on the sale of a depreciating asset that they were still paying on, but now they are not in a good position to move forward in the rental business. Lenders are watching; they want to make sure you're spending responsibly.

# Credibility and Accountability (Again)

Just like I mentioned in the last chapter, you should be accountable for all your personal and business decisions. I learned some hard lessons from my cheaper quotes and cheaper-in-the-moment fixes; cutting corners cost me more money in the long term than if I had simply fixed it correctly the first time. Cutting corners may save you hundreds of dollars in the present, but will ultimately cost you thousands in the future. That will add up to a pretty big sum of money if you make those mistakes—so hopefully, you've learned from mine instead.

Just like not cutting corners with maintenance or remodeling houses, you also never want to cut a corner when it comes to paperwork, because it can cost you just as much.

# Chapter 5
# Paperwork Matters

I'd purchased a property and inherited a tenant as a result. Eventually, I had to take that tenant to eviction court for a lease violation involving damage to the property. We had to go to court in order for me to take possession of the property and receive money for the damages. I had the minimum amount of paperwork required for our hearing...unfortunately, that didn't mean I had *all* the paperwork I needed.

Once proceedings were underway, I presented my side of the case and showed the lease, pictures of the damage, and invoices to the judge. I thought things were going well—until the tenant presented his side.

The tenant told the judge that he had never seen that lease and that the signed lease I'd presented did not contain his signature. Of course it was just a lie to try to get out of having to pay for the damages, but the judge then asked me who witnessed him signing this lease.

"I did, Your Honor," I replied.

"Do you have another form of ID with your signature?" the judge asked the tenant, and the tenant did.

The judge looked to see if the signatures matched up. They were a little off, but not by much. The tenant did sign the lease; however, the judge ended up ruling in the tenant's favor and dismissed the eviction action against him. He went on to recommend that, in the future, I get a copy of a tenant's photo ID and make sure their signatures match. I could not believe that my case was dismissed, and I could not believe that the judge ruled in the tenant's favor regarding the damages after such a lie. The tenant admitted that he lived at the property—so what happened?

## Prepare for the Worst and Hope for the Best

What I learned from that particular incident was that paperwork matters. Documentation matters. It's impossible to overthink this, because—even though I had documentation—I did not have a copy of the tenant's photo ID, and in the judge's mind, there was enough distinction between the two signatures to rule as he did.

Get prepared for court before you actually need to go to court. Make sure that you have your signed lease, a rental ledger, "before" photos of the property (and "after" photos, should any damage occur), and a paid invoice for any repairs. Always have a copy of the tenant's photo ID. After that day in court, I now take it a step further and take a photo of the tenant holding the lease so that I am never in this situation again.

Paperwork is not the most glamorous aspect of real estate, but it is one of the most important. Anything can happen, even if you are well prepared. Never leave an *i* undotted, nor *t* uncrossed; always have all the information you may need should you ever have to go to court. It doesn't matter whether you think something would be a straightforward case—it only matters whether the judge thinks so, and if you're not prepared, even overly prepared, you may lose. I speak from experience.

Now of course you could always appeal, but that will cost you more money. If you keep your paperwork in order, using the mindset that it may have to be presented in court someday, most likely you can avoid having to file an appeal. You really want to prepare like a lawyer would; when it comes to eviction-court proceedings, you might have to face an attorney, or the judge may ask you to produce some piece of documentation that seems random to you but could decide the case.

I can count on one hand how many cases were dismissed in the nine-plus years I have been in this business, but they all still sting when it happens.

Let me make a clear distinction about verbal and handshake agreements like I talked about in other chapters versus what I'm talking about in this chapter. Earlier, I spoke about forming authentic relationships with lenders and others who can help you find and finance properties. You will still have to have paperwork in order before you can do business with them; you may verbally agree or shake hands on a deal, but at some point, you will have to produce the correct documentation. It protects them, it protects you, and frankly, it demonstrates that you have a healthy respect for their profession.

This is not how you conduct yourself with tenants. Leases and landlord-tenant relationships are, in most cases, strictly transactional. You cannot risk a handshake or verbal agreement, and to do so puts you in a precarious position. It becomes a "he said-she said" situation, which does not bode well in court.

Normally, prospective tenants are very cordial and respectful when they need something from you, or when they are wanting to rent one of your properties for the first time; it doesn't always stay that way, especially if you have to file an eviction. Those verbal agreements and gentleman handshakes will not work for evictions related to damages to property. You must always prepare for the worst and hope for the best.

Get everything in writing, including the process and responsibilities for property damage. Make sure the lease clearly outlines the amount of rent, when it is due, how payments are to be made, and what happens when rent is past due. If you do not have it documented correctly, then the judge might rule against you. Make sure your lease details what the contract is, what the tenant is responsible for, and what the landlord is responsible for. Again, everyone will play nice in the beginning, but once you file eviction on someone, all bets are off.

# Get Your Systems in Place Before You Need Them

So far, I have covered (and yes, emphasized) why you need any tenant-related documents to be in order, but there are other types of paperwork that could eventually be used as supportive evidence in a court of law...or simply save you money.

Whether it's software warranties, maintenance contracts, insurance policies, process documents, or local tax receipts, know ahead of time that you need to keep up with these items before you purchase your first house or have a tenant sign a lease. It does not have to be a cluttered mess of files, and I will explain why. Let me take you through, step by step, how to prepare your paperwork.

## The Rental Process

In the rental process, you'll want documentation on the different advertisements used to promote properties that are available. Why would you keep up with that? In the event you're accused of discrimination, you'll have proof of how the property was advertised. Next, you'll want to keep all rental applications received and keep them locked and secure. We normally break down the applications by the month and keep them on file, even if we do not rent to the applicants.

Once we have decided to rent to the applicant, we make a copy of the application and keep one with all the other applications from that specific month, moving the second copy to a property file that will contain all the documents related to that property and that tenant, including the signed lease. Once the lease is filled out, verify that it matches the information written on the application, including the name(s), address(es), and emergency contact information. Confirm that those listed will be the individuals occupying the home, and—again—make sure the signatures match between the application and the lease, and I strongly encourage you to secure a copy of the photo IDs of all occupants except minor children. It seems like such a very small thing, but trust me, it can work against you if these items do not match. This way, if you ever have to go to court, you not only have the application, but you also have the lease and photo IDs. (As an added measure, we take a photograph of the lessee(s) holding the lease.)

Verbally review with the tenant what's written in their lease, particularly their responsibilities and yours. Part of that conversation should include late fees, which usually go into effect after the fifth of the month. Most late fees are 5 percent, but the terms of what happens when rent is late can be modified. You also want to make sure the tenant has a clear understanding of any sort of repair fees if the tenant causes damage.

If you allow pets, then you would want to charge an additional fee, and specify whether that's nonrefundable or what happens if the pet causes damage that costs more than the fee. All of this needs to be in writing; you are going over this with the tenant verbally as a courtesy.

I would recommend that you require your tenants to have renters insurance, and you'll want to review that section of the lease as well. Not only will renters insurance protect the tenant—it also protects you. Trust me, I learned the hard way about "recommending" instead of requiring renters insurance, and it has cost me thousands of dollars. Renters insurance really level-sets what the rental agreement truly is.

Take each of these steps before they are allowed to move in. If you are not local to the property or don't have a rental office, there are ways to do this virtually as well.

## Maintenance Contracts

It's important that maintenance contracts are very detailed. You want the contractor or handyman to understand the full scope of work and provide a detailed, itemized list of items included in that scope. You even want the total amount for each task itemized, and include a total at the bottom of the page.

You'll also need the payment terms spelled out in full, in writing. Trust me, when it comes to paying money, it can bring out the worst in anyone if you have to have a tough conversation. At least if you're faced with having one of those difficult conversations, you've already spelled out the terms and expectations up front. If you don't have it written on that document, you are putting yourself in a vulnerable position. A detailed contract not only protects you, but it also protects your handyman or contractor. You may have to have other types of conversations, but there should be no confusion about money and work expected—it makes the process much smoother. I would also keep warranty information with your maintenance contract, unless the warranty is specified in the contract itself.

## Insurance Policies

Your insurance policies—property insurance for all properties and general liability insurance—should be in order and reviewed each year. It is mutually beneficial for you and the insurance company to know what is covered, and that you have the right insurance on each property when you review them. You want to make sure that you have the right amount of insurance on the property in case it burns down or a tree falls on it, for example, and that you can build back the property with the amount of insurance you have. Or that you are covered if you experience a loss of rent, and what sorts of instances prompted that loss. If the property is down due to an insurance claim, then you will still receive rent for a reasonable time allotted for the property to be fixed. We'll take a deeper dive into insurance in Chapter Eight.

# Avoiding the Paper Tiger

Keeping all this paperwork is useless without a solid organization system. Otherwise, you'll waste hours, if not days, searching for documents when you need them.

If you choose a paper system, make sure copies are made, and place the originals in a secure, fireproof, waterproof filing cabinet, and keep it locked unless you are using it. All sensitive and pertinent documents, including leases, applications, maintenance contracts, warranties, and insurance policies, should be kept in this cabinet.

There are software programs that can also keep you organized, whether it's rental collection software or software that helps you keep track of rent and tenant ledgers. Even if you opt for a paper system for daily use, you want that stuff to be backed up on a computer or in a cloud drive—whatever you need to do to keep it safe, secure, and accessible by you.

If you work with an IT company, they can help you back up your files for safekeeping. You want to keep everything protected, whether that is your computer software, passwords, your private information, and that of your tenants. If any tenant's information is compromised, you could be held liable for that breach.

If you do not have a solid filing system to keep all these items straight, you are not going to be productive, and it will be hard to keep track of everything. Take the time to get it right and in the long run, it will make you more money instead of costing you thousands. When I first got into the business, I only thought I was organized; looking back, I was not as organized as I needed to be, which cost me several thousands of dollars, because it was a scramble if I had to file an eviction or chase down late rental payments...because there again, contracts matter and paperwork matters.

# Don't Make It Up As You Go Along

Why is it a bad idea to just make it up as you go along? After all, when you're just starting out, it's one property. It's not like you're going to come out of the chute with three hundred rental properties and no gameplan...right?

Believe me, there is plenty that you cannot anticipate as a landlord or as a real estate investor. If you have systems in place before you need them, then your life and business become a lot easier when something goes wrong, or when you need something. If you do not do this correctly, it could cost you thousands of dollars; if you do it correctly, however, it can ultimately make you thousands more.

When I think about people who make it up as they go along, it makes me think they are running a business on a whim, which is a recipe for disaster. You want things to be thought out and thought through. As exciting as real estate investing can be, you need to come back down to Earth and anticipate what could potentially go wrong, and formulate possible solutions before you need them. You should have processes and systems in place not only to protect yourself from liabilities but also to protect the direction you're headed when something does go wrong. When your emotions are running high, you might not be thinking clearly; if you have your systems in place, you can craft a response instead of a reaction. You'll know how to handle certain situations before you need to, and before you become emotional. That will help you be more successful and make better, more sound decisions long term.

# The Probability Factor

Some of you may not be convinced. You're thinking, This will never happen to me. I'm renting my garage apartment to my best friend's son while he attends college. No chance we'll have issues.

If I had only slowed down and thought about other outcomes that could have happened in that court case, it would not have cost me thousands of dollars. Maybe you have been fortunate so far, but there will be times when your fortune runs thin or runs out completely. You can't anticipate everything, nor can you predict the future, but the more time you can spend sealing the soft spots, the better prepared you will be. Having your paperwork in order and systems in place will help you navigate those situations that you thought would "never" happen.

# Chapter 6
# Maintenance

I had a company put LVP flooring in a bathroom. When I inspected the job, I could tell just by walking on it that it was not installed correctly—there were still soft spots. I had to call the company back to fix it and get it right, but the delay cost me time and money. It was a great learning experience for both the flooring company and myself about validating the work that was done.

It's the old saying: trust, but verify.

The person who installed the flooring needed to understand the correct way to install it and the importance of getting it right the first time. Had I not inspected the work myself, I would have been paying to have it replaced again in the near future. So while the reinstall cost me more money and time, it could have cost me a lot more money and time had I overlooked it or not checked it out myself.

And frankly, I also know that I'm fortunate that the flooring company was willing to come back and correct the work; in most cases, companies will not come back out if they have already been paid. That's why it is always important to verify the work that was done before you cut a check. I know some vendors are calling to get paid as they're driving in the last nail, but you always want to lay your eyes on the work before paying.

With that lesson learned, I had a different property that had a leak in the kitchen sink, which caused a few soft spots in the flooring. I had a maintenance service pull the floor and the cabinets to make the necessary repairs to the leak, make the necessary repairs to the soft spots in the subfloor, put the cabinets back in place, and then install LVP. This job was 100 percent handled correctly, and no corners were cut. That was over five years ago; the floor still looks brand-new, the property has been very low-maintenance, and we've had zero issues with leaks.

What made the difference between the two scenarios? With the first property, I had some assumptions that a flooring company would do everything to make it right. Learn from my hard-earned lesson: assuming anything in this business is the worst mistake you can make.

You always want to explain what you want done, and get as detailed as possible. Was it absolutely necessary to rip out the cabinets just to fix a leak? Some of you may be thinking, *It's just a rental property*, but let me remind you that while it's not your primary residence, it will be somebody else's. Sure, it was a lot of work and perhaps to an outsider looking in, it may have seemed like a bit of overkill, but we repaired it right the first time, and five years later, that decision has not only saved me money; it has made me money. Maintenance on that property has been minimal, and there have been zero repairs, which would have cut into the profits.

If things are handled correctly the first time and properly maintained, they will last.

# Maintenance versus Repairs

What is the difference between maintenance and repairs? It's actually fairly simple.

Preventative maintenance includes those things you do in order to prevent further issues and keep the property value up: mowing the yard, trimming the shrubs, keeping the house pressure-washed and clean, routine maintenance on HVAC systems, and so on. You usually have maintenance items on a schedule, whether it's annual, quarterly, monthly, even weekly.

Repairs, on the other hand, are not routine and do not follow a regular schedule. Many times, repairs are caused by neglect, unless it's caused by something like a natural disaster. Leaks are fairly common repairs, whether they are leaks from a roof, sink, or toilet.

Think of it like this: Maintenance is proactive. Repairs are reactive.

Maintenance can be easy...or hard. If you are proactive and have a good vendor list for anything and everything that could potentially happen to the property, maintenance will be easy.

- Time to clean out the gutters? You've got a vendor for that, and a backup vendor if the first one is busy.
- Time to reseal a driveway? You've got a vendor for that, and a backup vendor if the first one is busy.
- Time to do HVAC maintenance? You've got a vendor for that, and a backup vendor if the first one is busy.

Most maintenance is preventative. You do it to either prevent larger repairs or minimize a repair that may reveal itself through regular maintenance. For example, regular upkeep of shrubbery and trees will prevent branches from scratching up siding or causing roof leaks. Resealing and recaulking toilets and tubs will prevent water damage. Regular HVAC maintenance alerts you to any repairs or parts that need replacing (and changing the filters regularly prevents the entire HVAC system from wearing out).

The more proactive you are about maintenance, the better the outcome; you will have a happy tenant and protect your asset.

Maintenance becomes hard if you don't have a vendor list or if you have the mindset that "it's just a rental property" and decide to neglect the issue or cut corners. That mindset will cost you thousands more and create a huge headache for you.

Having a vendor list or a maintenance team before you actually need a vendor or a maintenance team is a huge deal. Whether that means hiring a full-time maintenance person or handyman or having a third-party vendor for HVAC, electrical work, plumbing, roofing, etc., you want a go-to list already in place before something goes wrong. And if they are already handling regular maintenance items, they are more likely to work with you when repairs become necessary. If you do not have a team in place, this business will become extremely hard for you.

Depending on how many properties you own, it may be more cost-effective for you to put someone, or several someones, on your payroll. This can be a full-time maintenance manager, or a contracted handyman and other vendors. If you're just starting out, this would be a very expensive option, but as you continue to grow and scale your rental business, I would then look at potentially bringing someone on full-time who can go wherever you need them immediately if something goes wrong. If you start accumulating maybe thirty to forty units, then I would start looking at having someone on payroll—whether that person is part-time or full-time—to handle your maintenance requests. There is a threshold where that becomes more cost-effective for you and provides better service for your tenants.

Now earlier, I mentioned having backup vendors if your regular vendors are unavailable or cannot get to you in a timely manner. When something goes wrong, it could be a very stressful moment, and you might not be thinking clearly. This is why you plan ahead of time and have a vendor list with service providers you have established relationships with; if you're not thinking clearly, and your go-to isn't available, you don't want to put yourself in a desperate position where you are overcharged for substandard repairs. Get your backup vendors in place.

Remember, in this business, relationships are key. If someone is already handling regular maintenance and something urgent occurs, they are more likely to stop what they're doing and make your situation a priority. You have established and grown that relationship, so you matter to them as much as they matter to you. You also want to establish relationships with backup vendors; you never want to rely on one plumber or one handyman exclusively. Just like you do business with more than one lender, you want to "spread the joy," so to speak, when it comes to your maintenance team; otherwise, you're beholden to them, their schedule, and so on. It's a balancing act, for sure.

# What Must Be Maintained?

It's beyond the scope of this book to get into items pervasive to a specific property, but there are some maintenance items that are, in fact, universal to any property.

On an as-needed basis, make sure:

- the yard stays mowed;
- bushes and trees stay away from the house and don't mess up the roof line; and
- the roof remains in good shape.

Make sure the HVAC system is serviced on a yearly basis and filters are changed according to the manufacturer's instructions.

On a semiannual or quarterly basis, inspect the properties for any preventative maintenance or repairs.

Check for leaks or loose components on the following:

- the kitchen sink
- bathroom sinks
- toilets and bathtubs
- plumbing fixtures

Check electrical outlets to make sure the tenants aren't overloading them.

Walk around the outside of the property to make sure, from foundation to the roof, everything seems to be solid and sealed. If you allow pets, walk around the yard to make sure they are disposing of any pet waste properly.

We try to do inspections on every property every six months, but it's really up to you as to how often you want to conduct them. This also holds your tenant accountable for anything that they might be tearing up during the time that they live there. Refer to their lease, or make sure you have a maintenance addendum on the lease that specifies what is required for you to take care of and what is required for your tenant to take care of, as they should pay for any repairs that are the result of their negligence.

Now sometimes, a vendor discovers there is more to the repair than originally scoped. For example, a leaky faucet may be linked to further damage. I always tell the vendor up front, before they go to the property, that if they find further damage, they are to pick up the phone and call me immediately. I will either meet the vendor over at the property to look at what they discovered, or I will have the vendor take pictures and text them over to me. This way, you are confirming what the vendor is telling you and you're also getting an accurate picture—because some people do not explain the magnitude of what the further damage could be, and sometimes seeing it for yourself is best. You can assess the situation and decide how you want to handle it, whether that means letting the vendor who is there fix it or having another vendor come in and fix it.

Remember—trust, but verify.

Maintaining properties correctly protects your assets, gives you the reputation for renting nicer homes, and usually gives you less to do when you have a tenant turnover.

# Maintenance and Repair Schedules

How far in advance do you need to schedule maintenance? It really depends on how far in advance you need to contact the vendor, particularly if they stay booked, or if you have a large job for them to do. If it's time to replace a roof, windows, or HVAC system, for example, you would want to plan these things out in advance with the vendors. These require full days or more to install, and they need to be able to work them into their schedules. They are not true emergencies; they are larger maintenance jobs.

How far in advance do you need to schedule repairs? Those usually cannot wait. If you have a leaky sink, for example, or a heat system is out and it's a forty-degree day, those things cannot wait, and a vendor should be contacted immediately (trust me, water damage is devastating, and landlord-tenant law specifies that you must provide an adequate heat source). The vendor will understand if these are true emergencies, and the priority of tending to them; you do need to expect to pay a premium price, however, if you are asking them to stop what they are doing to prioritize your needs.

Using our earlier examples, if your roof or windows are leaking or your HVAC system is not working, then those would be considered emergencies. Normally, however, a roofer can tarp your roof in the event of storm damage, which would hold until they can get you worked in.

How far in advance do you need to notify the tenant about any maintenance and repair items, and then, do you only notify them once? When scheduling maintenance, you want to at least give your tenant a minimum twenty-four-hour notice. If it is not an emergency, most leases will require this, but if your lease requires a more advanced notice, you need to abide by the terms of the lease—because if you're going to hold your tenant accountable to the lease, you also need to hold yourself to that lease. Regardless, if you can provide them with more than twenty-four hours' notice, that's even better; it shows that you respect their time and privacy and gives them more time to prepare in case furniture needs to be moved or they need to be there at the time.

In an emergency situation, most leases allow you to take immediate access and not provide a notice, because you have the right to protect your property. I would still give the tenant a call, text, or email to let them know that maintenance will be coming by. Normally, if it's an emergency, this will not be an issue because likely, the tenant was the one who alerted you in the first place.

# Documentation

Part of managing maintenance also involves managing documentation. You always want to keep good records of maintenance work that was done to the property and have a good filing system that allows you to look up previous maintenance work on individual properties and units.

What sorts of documents should you keep? All estimates or invoices for work that was completed on the property. Always keep the written estimate so that you know the price that was agreed upon to do the work, and then once the work is completed, you can compare the invoice with the estimate to make sure they align. Keep in mind that if additional work had to be done, that may not be reflected on the original estimate.

This way, you have two documents showing what the estimate was going to be and what it actually cost to complete. Keep these files for tax purposes, and so that you can recall the last time work was done and who did it. Trust me, you don't want to try and remember all that information in your head!

Keeping up with maintenance and repair documentation is critical because at the end of the day, we are taking all the rents that come in, minus expenses...and what's left is your profit. If you're missing documentation, then you cannot effectively see whether you are turning a profit, and you won't remember when maintenance was last performed or if there is a warranty included with the work. Even a trusted vendor can get it wrong at times.

If maintenance records are not properly kept, it could cost you tens of thousands of dollars. For example, if your roofer said your roof comes with a five-year warranty and you do not keep the invoice and keep the records organized, and the roof starts to leak within five years, then you might have to pay out of pocket to have that roof repaired. Whereas if you kept good records, you could have the roofer come back out and make those repairs for you, because you would have the proper documentation. New HVAC systems normally all come with a warranty, but if you do not keep good records of when the HVAC system was installed, and your maintenance records are not up to date, you cannot prove that your unit is still under warranty...and you might have to pay out of pocket for those repairs.

If you have proper documentation, you might still have to pay for the labor, but the parts would be covered under the warranty and be free. New HVAC systems can have bad compressors installed, for example—there's no way of knowing—and compressors are a pricey way to learn that you should have kept up with the warranty paperwork.

In addition, if you do not have documents supporting your expenses at the end of the year for tax purposes, you will not be able to deduct them. I promise that the IRS will not take your word for it.

Finally, documentation may be important if you ever have to go to court. For example, if you have to take a tenant to court seeking damages, you will need evidence to back up your claims, and these documents would support your case. Or if the tenant takes you to court, repairs and maintenance documentation can help you for the exact same reason. Otherwise, you may be penalized, or the case could be thrown out.

# Settling Up

Once the work is complete, the vendor should hand over an invoice and any sort of warranty work or paperwork that comes with it. Normally, you will receive warranty information when it comes to a roof or HVAC system, but for flooring or carpet, you might not. There is no harm in asking for a warranty, of course, but you will want them to provide an invoice that outlines the work that was completed, and you'll want that bill itemized as well. This will help you later if a vendor ever claims they weren't paid for a certain portion of the work. A detailed invoice fully outlines the scope of the work that was done, and protects you from a vendor coming back years down the road stating that you did not pay in full.

Now when it comes to payment, if you have an estimate and an invoice in hand, then it becomes a lot easier to get vendors paid. I always ask vendors to review their estimate with me and let me know exactly what it covers. That way, there is no confusion. One of the questions I always ask is "When do you need to get paid?"

The one thing that always gets people upset is not being paid, and nothing can take you down quicker than a reputation of not paying your bills. You always want to do right by your vendors and follow the payment terms specified on the invoice, because some people are paid upon completion, others want to be paid within seven days, and others will give you thirty days. Get the payment terms up front.

I have mentioned that you want to compare the estimate to the invoice to ensure they are correct and align with each other. If they do not align, it is perfectly okay to ask questions. Most vendors have no issue walking you through this to help you understand; remember, they run a business too and have a reputation to consider. So always ask questions, but do it in a way that creates a good relationship between you and the vendor.

Never pay a vendor before seeing the work in person. There are going to be vendors that you work with that want to be paid the same day that the work is completed and will pressure you; I do not recommend that you pay without seeing the finished product. I'm speaking from experience; early in my career, I was pressured to pay vendors before seeing the work that was done, and the work was subpar. Since I'd already paid, there wasn't much recourse I could take with them, and I still had to find someone else to go in and fix the problems they left. Don't put yourself in that situation; discuss the payment terms up front, but also tell the vendor what you will be doing once the work is complete, so there is no confusion.

# Can't Insurance Pay for This?

Why should you put so much time and effort into regular maintenance, or even minor repairs? Shouldn't you just wait until something breaks and file an insurance claim?

None of this is on autopilot. Maintenance takes a lot of time, but it is necessary. I do not recommend waiting until everything breaks to fix things, much less counting on insurance to cover something. Trust me, that will be an even bigger expense.

It doesn't cost that much money to do preventative maintenance to properties after you have performed an inspection. Cost-wise, it will be far more manageable. Sure, there will be things that you just wait until they break before replacing—roof, HVAC, and so on. But that doesn't mean you neglect them in the meantime. Roofs should be clear of debris and regularly checked for leaks or soft spots, and gutters should be cleaned. The HVAC system should have regular maintenance performed, at a minimum, once a year. In those cases, only do repairs if it is causing damage to the property.

Now, if a storm comes through and damages your roof, your insurance company can help pay to have it replaced. But if an HVAC system goes out, the insurance company might not pay for that unless it was storm-related damage, and that would depend on the types of coverage you have. So if your property has a thirty-year-old HVAC system, I would say start planning for its replacement, but do not replace it until it goes out.

Remember, there is a difference between preventative maintenance and repairs. It would be a waste of money to make repairs or replace things that are not broken.

Your insurance policy isn't a guaranteed safety net for repairs. Insurance claims also take time. Once you file a claim, it can be several days before an adjuster reaches out to schedule a time to come see the damage; then, it would be a couple more days before they can actually arrive, and the insurance company has to review what the adjuster sends in...the actual repair could take a while. In addition, the more insurance claims that you file may result in a higher premium—and you want to keep insurance premiums affordable. Only use insurance for what the insurance actually covers, and avoid filing claims thinking it's a cheaper way to pay for major repairs.

# Maintenance Is Cheaper than Repairs

At the beginning of this chapter, I offered two examples of work being handled wrong and work being handled correctly. The difference between the two, and what I learned from both of them, is that you have to communicate clearly—do not assume anything, and always follow up once the work is completed.

Remember—trust, but verify.

Even a vendor you've used for a long time, one that normally does a good job for you, may have a new hire who tries to cut a corner and not do it correctly. Always verify that the work is done correctly. In the long run, this will save you time and money, and you'll have a much better product, a better-quality rental, and happy tenants.

Preventative maintenance is cheaper than making repairs, so stay a step ahead on it. You never know when something that you did not plan for is going to happen, and if your property is well maintained, you will be in a better position to handle the "unexpecteds."

# Chapter 7
# Prepare for the Unthinkable

I always knew not to expect every tenant to pay on time, all the time; then the pandemic happened. Tenants did not have to pay rent for close to two years, because the government put a freeze on filing evictions for nonpayment of rent.

It was a very difficult situation for everyone. No one thought that the world was going to shut down, and certainly no one thought that the government was going to put a freeze on filing evictions on tenants for nonpayment of rent...not for two years, anyway. But they did.

During that time, a lot of landlords wondered how they were going to make ends meet. Fortunately, since the government put a freeze on evictions for nonpayment of rent, they also gave help to tenants that needed help paying their rent. In the state of North Carolina, there was a program called the HOPE Program that helped tenants pay their rent. You could get almost a year and a half's worth of rent paid if you filed the correct paperwork through the proper channels. This was still a very difficult moment because tenants were the ones who had to file everything and it was up to them, not the landlord, to be able to file.

Yes, the unthinkable had happened. I was blessed during this time because most of my tenants took advantage of the HOPE Program. The majority of the rent was paid for almost two years, if they needed the assistance. Nonetheless, it took a lot of work and a lot of organization to keep track of it all.

I was fortunate—other landlords coming out of the pandemic were not. During that time, I received most of my rent; a lot of landlords did not receive most of the rent they were owed, because their tenants did not do what they were supposed to do, and they did not get help that they could have received.

# One Step Ahead

Thinking about the unthinkables keeps you one step ahead. This definitely rang true in this situation, because even pre-pandemic, I had the forethought that I could not count on all of my tenants paying their rent at the same time. I could not have predicted that *none* of them would pay, however, and certainly not for two years, but I had enough of a head start to quickly pivot on the rest.

It would be very hard to prepare for a pandemic that most in this generation have never seen before, and certainly not of this magnitude— but it was a good lesson and reminder to prepare for the unthinkable. You cannot control what might happen, but you can control the response and have policies in place to take care of that...or at least, soften the blow.

Coming out of the pandemic, my company is now prepared for the next pandemic or anything similar. Yes, we were fortunate; but that doesn't mean we overlook the lessons we learned. Now we have planned ahead, and we will be able to navigate those situations even better.

Prepare for other instances and circumstances that you also think will *never* happen, because if the coronavirus pandemic taught us anything, we now know it certainly could.

# Negative Outlook?

I consider myself a positive thinker, and I look for the best in most situations. But I disagree with those who say that thinking about negative things or things that will "never" happen is not the right mindset.

You become a better leader and run a better business when you prepare for things that can go wrong, because bad things always happen. Yes, I still find the good in most situations, but I also prepare for the bad situations because I live in the real world that has flaws; preparing this way makes me a better business owner, landlord, and CEO of a business where people rely on me for their livelihoods.

Learn from history instead of eliminating history, because most of the time, history does repeat itself. I have had quite a few things go wrong over the years, most of which I had no control over, but I was prepared to handle them, including the following:

- COVID-19 pandemic
- house fires
- tenants breaking back into homes post-eviction and retaliating

Even writing this book, my original publisher suddenly closed, and that left me wondering if I would ever get this book published. In all of these difficult circumstances, I had prepared. And honestly, I think that keeps me from "going negative" in a negative situation.

Sometimes you can only prepare through experience, but I challenge you to think about what might go wrong...and prepare for it.

For example, what if the fire department called you right now and said one of your rental houses is on fire. What would be your first response? What would you do in that situation? How would you handle it? A fire is something that could happen to anyone...including landlords. Fires happen every day all over the world, and it could happen to you, too.

I would challenge you to have some of those answers already in place, even if it is just a basic plan of response, and what the next step might look like. That way, if and when you are in that moment—which will be an emotional time—you already have decisions in place that were thought through when you were more rational and calm. The best way to do that is to "pre-think" about some of the bad things that could potentially happen.

# A Strategic Approach

When I received a call from the fire department informing me that one of my properties caught on fire, my initial response was "Is everyone okay?" It was not about the property—it was about making sure that human life was taken care of, and that everyone was safe.

The reason why I responded that way was because, for one thing, I'm a human and care about human life, but two, I was prepared for something like this, should it ever happen. I already knew that my insurance would cover the property, so the property should not be my immediate concern...let me think about what is *not* covered. By doing that, my focus was solely on the tenants and making sure they had a place to go, and making sure they had some money to replace some of the items and daily essentials that they needed.

In this particular case, I helped the tenants get a few items and set them up in a hotel for a few days while they transitioned to living elsewhere. By being prepared, I could focus on the things that mattered, and I was not super emotional about any of it—I had a clear head because I'd already thought this process through.

No, I didn't wake up every day thinking, *What if today is the day one of my properties burns to the ground?* and stay fearful all day, worrying about it. I didn't think it was likely that it would ever happen to me, but that doesn't mean I ignored it; I mean, a fire was not likely, but it was possible. Humans make mistakes.

One thing that I did learn through this process was to require tenants to have renters insurance. My company makes sure that every tenant has a policy, because renters insurance not only protects you as the property owner, but it protects the tenant even more for situations that are unthinkable—like a house fire.

Remember—trust, but verify. This strategy applies here, too.

I use that strategy because of the experience I have gained being in this business. I have learned that not everyone is going to do the right thing, or do it the way you would want them to. Not everyone is going to have the same standards as you. So when it comes to tenants, landlords, local government agencies, or local nonprofit agencies that are paying people's rents, I always trust what they are saying, but I verify as well.

This is critical when it comes to tenants. They don't always tell you the truth. I call this "tenant talk" because I have so many tenants that have lied to me over the years. You have to keep in mind that what they're saying may be their version of the truth, but not the real truth. When a tenant says that they are going to pay rent on the fifth of the month, for example, trust that their word means something, but verify that they actually put the money in on the fifth—because this could be potential tenant talk.

Say the grass is high at a property, and you have called your lawn company to cut it, and they say they're going to cut it by Friday. On Friday, verify that the grass has been cut by either going by the property yourself or having the tenant or lawn care company send you a picture of it freshly cut. This way, you are trusting the lawn care company, but you are also verifying that they have kept their word.

So while I trust what most people tell me is the truth, I also verify that what they are telling me is correct. You never want to take someone's word for it, because there again, most people are not for you. If you apply the "trust, but verify" strategy to prepare for the unthinkable, you will always put yourself in a better situation and hopefully avoid putting yourself in any bad ones.

# Balance and Repetition

So what happens when a tenant has lied to you about something that was their fault, and it cost you? For example, what happens when they dent an appliance and claim they didn't do it? Or windows are broken out, and they don't know how it happened? Causes of fires are fairly easy to determine, but other issues are not as easy to prove. This is a tightrope walk, because I have had to call tenants out on lies before, but when push comes to shove, and dollars come to cents, can I prove some of these, beyond a shadow of a doubt? No.

And tenants who are savvy know this. I'm not talking about regular maintenance or normal wear and tear—I'm talking about repeat damages, or damage that is detrimental to your property.

It's a balancing act, however. With tenant talk, if you know what to look for, know how to verify, then you also need to know that sometimes, you are just going to have to pay, even though you know the tenant is lying. If you cannot prove something, you can't force them to pay for it.

History always repeats itself, even if it's years down the road. We can hope the next time it does, we are better prepared than the last time. In the rental business, you will always have a tenant who pays every single month, on time, when they say they're going to pay. And then on the flip side of that, you will always have a tenant who says they are going to pay, and they never do. Lather, rinse, repeat. That doesn't really change, but the more units that you have, it does amplify what you might have.

Say you have five units, then you might have one bad tenant that creates an issue. If you have one hundred tenants, then you might have ten bad tenants. History repeats itself, because some of the same issues will continue to resurface, month after month. That's just the rental business in general; sometimes, it's very challenging. Knowing how to balance, and knowing that there will be repetition will help you manage things long term.

# The Unexpecteds and Unthinkables

I have mentioned several scenarios of unexpecteds and unthinkables that have happened to me during my years in the rental business; I have also underscored that you need to be prepared as best you can for those hiccups. But how do we do this without a crystal ball?

If a tenant completely trashes your house before you file an eviction, for example, or before the eviction process is over, how do you prepare for that? Or if they left a bunch of stuff inside the property, how do you handle that? You would have no way of knowing in advance that this was going to happen.

This is a great reason to already have vendors lined up. You can call a vendor to clean the house out, patch holes in the walls, and so on. Just like you have a list of painters who may paint or touch up a unit each time it's turned over, that same painter may be able to take care of business when disaster strikes. This will also help you remain calm because, let's face it, a tenant trashing your property is upsetting.

If a tenant were to break back into the property post-eviction, how do you handle that? Again, it's upsetting because you would hope that they would move along and leave well enough alone. Since they've chosen to retaliate, I would call the police immediately, file a police report, and then make sure that you have vendors in place who can come fix the broken door or window that allowed them access to the property. They can come and rescue your house for you.

By doing the small things and being prepared, that will help you handle those situations better—because I promise you, your blood pressure will be elevated, along with your heart rate. That's an understandable reaction, but since you have policies in place on how to handle certain situations, you can manage it. I have found that these situations end a lot better when you have those decisions in place *before* your emotions are high.

What if you do everything right and you still get taken? How will any previous preparation help lessen that blow? Look, there will always be things that you do correctly, and you still get taken advantage of, or the outcome is not what you wanted. For example, we have a policy in place where we file evictions on certain days of the month. When that takes place, we communicate with the tenant and let them know that we will be filing eviction. There is always a time or two every year where a tenant asks for just a few more days to get the rent paid. Obviously, we are human and understand that things come up; sometimes, we allow people a few extra days. We have done this more times than I would like to count.

Those tenants will sometimes take advantage of that situation and not do the right thing. "A few more days" turns into a few weeks because we did not follow our eviction plan accordingly. We did not follow the eviction plan accordingly because we wanted to give the tenants a little more time, because we are human. Sometimes, that backfires.

In the past, we had tenants we were working with to pay rent and we let them know, "Hey, if you go ahead and move out, we won't file an eviction." And instead, they left a complete mess in these instances, taking advantage of us when we were actually helping them by not filing and having that on their records. We did everything the right way from a business standpoint and a human-being standpoint, but the tenant still took advantage of the situation.

There are also situations where the tenant causes something like a house fire, which is what happened to me. They completely destroyed a property, and there was no way to prepare for that kind of damage—except that I had a process in place for getting them to a safe place, getting the fire addressed, and knowing who I needed to call to get the insurance company out there quickly.

With a procedure in place "in the unlikely event," I did everything right—but I was still not able to do anything about the property being destroyed and tenants being without a home, beyond the temporary housing of a hotel. There wasn't anything else I could have done differently in that situation to make for any better outcome, but we were able to move quickly to get our ducks in a row. It took months to rebuild the house. The tenants were out of their belongings, and we were able to provide them some money so they could go buy clothes and a few items while putting them up in a hotel. But there again, even when you plan for the unthinkable and do everything right, sometimes it is extremely hard to get through that tough situation.

# What You Can and Cannot Control

When you lead a company, it's ultimately all on your shoulders. People are counting on you. And I do not take that lightly.

It is within your control to think about different possibilities that could potentially happen and be prepared for them. Write them down, along with how you would handle certain situations. Even though the next big "unexpected" that comes up may not be the exact scenario you wrote down, you still have an advantage because you are not starting from scratch, nor learning as you go. The only thing you can control is how you react to a situation. You can't control what happens to you, but you can certainly control how you respond. That is why it is so important to think about things that could potentially happen, even if it's really far-fetched. Be prepared, think through things thoroughly. Ask other landlords about their experiences or what they would recommend, in terms of preparation.

You cannot control tenants tearing up properties, people not paying rent, a house fire, a pandemic...and many, many more situations and circumstances. Don't focus on trying to control these things, because you will never be able to put your focus on what you can control going forward.

I do not tell you all of this to scare you, but I want you to be prepared. I am so grateful for all the experiences I have had, good and bad, because they have made me a better leader, landlord, and person. I am grateful to have great tenants over the years—even the few tenants that did bad things. Those bad ones never outweigh the good ones. I know how blessed I am to have as many good tenants as I do, and I will challenge you to be grateful for the same.

I promise that if you only focus on the bad and problematic, you will hate this business and not enjoy it. Just like with anything in life, your mindset is everything. If you focus on the good, that tends to be more gratifying, because you can see the blessings you have in life. But if you turn your focus on the bad, that will make you bitter and not let you realize how blessed you are. I always tell people to "never say never" and to always be prepared—the unthinkable *can* happen, because it *has* happened over the years.

When I first got into this business, I never thought I would have a property burn down or a tenant who trashed my property; but I did. Again, do not live in fear of what might happen. Just have a gameplan for how you might handle these things; you can't control them happening to you, but you can certainly control your response to it and manage what happens.

# Save for a Rainy Day

The issue we ran into with nonpayment during the pandemic could have been devastating, but we actually had some success. We took what was happening to us in the moment and practically created a real-time plan to still be successful. Sure, it would have been easier to just make excuses that this was just too hard, and it was unfair; I promise you, though, life isn't fair, and business isn't always fair either. You have to play the cards that you were dealt.

Most of our tenants signed up for assistance and had their rent paid during that time. We were not hit as hard as most people, but it still took a lot of work to get us there. Post-pandemic, most people were still struggling; landlords had to evict a lot of people for nonpayment, and we had our fair share of evictions as well, but at least we did not get hit twice—one for nonpayment during COVID, and two for nonpayment post-COVID, plus having to evict people for nonpayment of rent. If we did not have the HOPE Program paying tenants during COVID, we would have been in trouble—just like most people in the rental business, or in business in general. Thankfully, we are past that, and we are back to thriving instead of surviving.

As I've mentioned, my parents used to tell me to save for a rainy day, because the rain always comes. Rain certainly came during the pandemic, and if we hadn't made business decisions years in advance, then we might not be here today, still in business.

I always tell people to protect themselves against situations that they think could happen and that almost never happen, because you never know. It's so important to protect yourself this way; and one very important way to do that is to ensure that you have good insurance.

# Chapter 8
# Insurance, Trusts, and Protecting Your Assets

Once, I was sued personally by a tenant because I did not return their security deposit due to damages. The tenant filed the paperwork against me personally, and it clearly showed in their lease that the property was owned by an LLC. So when I went into court, as soon as the judge swore us both in, I made a motion for dismissal, because the tenant sued me personally, and I do not own the property personally—it is owned by an LLC, and according to the law, you cannot sue someone personally for it. You have to sue the LLC. At the judge's request, I provided documentation, and the judge immediately dismissed the action against me.

The moral of the story: if the property was in my personal name, then the judge would have heard the case. Had I lost, then the person would have a judgment against me personally and could have potentially come after my personal assets.

## Protect Your Business and Protect Yourself

The key to being successful long term in this business is protection—not only of your investment properties but also your personal assets. You need to have an LLC set up, property insurance, and general liability insurance to protect yourself from the unknowns.

You never want to put yourself in a vulnerable position, if it's within your control. Protect yourself by never owning rental property in your personal name. Make sure that you have the right general liability insurance in place to support protecting your business and your LLC.

If someone sued me through the LLC, then my general liability coverage would have kicked in to help defend me. Fortunately, in this case, the tenant filed it incorrectly and it was dismissed, but had it been filed correctly, I had extra protections in place to protect my business and mitigate the cost, if necessary.

Now, to make sure you understand, I am not talking about skirting responsibility or cheating anyone here. Anyone can sue anybody for anything. It's as simple as going down to the courthouse, filling out the proper paperwork, and paying a certain amount of money. You actually don't have to do anything wrong to be sued. In the case I mentioned, I was sued because a tenant did not like my decision, even though their lease clearly stated what I was communicating to them.

Do not allow fear of being sued to stop you from going after your dreams. I have been sued countless times during my career in this business, and if you're in business long enough, you will be, too. If you have the right protections in place, and you are conducting business correctly, you will have a great defense. More times than not, those actions will either be dismissed or ruled in your favor.

When it comes to protecting yourself personally and professionally, you want to be proactive. You do not want to be reactive to this, so have these items in place before you actually need them. I have all of my properties in an LLC, and general liability insurance that covers the LLC and the properties; I also have an umbrella policy that provides extra protection for me personally.

Once you have been sued, yes, you could still move them into an LLC at that point—but that LLC is not going to protect you against that particular lawsuit. And no insurance policy will cover you if you have already been sued, and the policy is not already in place. Be proactive—get these items in place before you actually need them, even before you move your first tenant into one of your properties.

# How to Protect Yourself

There are different ways to protect yourself and your business. We have taken several chapters to mention why LLCs are important—they protect you against the unknown, protect you against situations completely out of your control, and prevent someone from taking something that is not owned within the LLC, like your personal home. Consult with your local attorney and accountant to make sure you set up the correct one.

Now I have taken this a step further and set up two LLCs. One LLC owns my rental properties, and another LLC manages them. This adds an additional layer of protection. The LLC that owns the properties enters into a rental management agreement with the other.

The rental management agreement states that the LLC that owns the properties permits the rental management LLC to rent out the properties, which adds that extra layer of protection. The rental management company doesn't have any assets, so they assume all the liabilities by renting out the properties to tenants. So if a tenant sues, they have to sue the rental management company, which doesn't have any assets; they cannot sue the LLC that owns the properties, because they are not the ones renting them out to the tenants.

Yes, there is more work and expense up front to do it this way, but it's really not that much when you consider the long-term benefits. This arrangement could save you thousands down the road.

You can also protect your personal assets by setting up a trust. I strongly recommend that you consult with an attorney who handles them to find out whether this is the best way to protect your personal assets. For me, a trust was my best option.

I put several different things within the trust, including property I do not rent out that is reserved for my personal use. That way, if something occurs in my personal life, like a car accident or some such, and someone sues me personally, they cannot come after my personal assets because they are protected by the trust.

How does that work?

When assets are protected by the trust, this means that I technically do not own whatever is placed within the trust; instead, I am considered a trustee. Heaven forbid I accidentally hurt someone while driving a car and they are injured, but if they sue me personally, then that person could come after my car. My car is in my personal name, and my personal general liability insurance will also help protect me, but I do not own anything else in my name. So they would not be able to come after my home, because that has been placed in the trust. You never want one mistake or one instance to take away everything you have worked so hard for.

There are several different types of trusts available, but the two most commonly arranged are a revocable trust and an irrevocable trust. They are different, so it is very important that you understand how each one works before you move anything into a trust. It is a legal arrangement that you can use to manage and distribute your property either during your lifetime or once you pass away.

A revocable trust can be changed at any time by the grantor during their lifetime, as long as they are competent. An irrevocable trust usually cannot be changed without a court order or the approval of the trust beneficiaries. This makes an irrevocable trust less flexible, but an irrevocable trust can protect assets from certain creditors and estate taxes while a revocable trust cannot.

The person creating a trust is called a grantor. Once a grantor creates a trust, they fund it by transferring their assets to the trust. They will also name a trustee to manage the trust assets and choose beneficiaries for the trust. Property beneficiaries are the people or organizations who will receive assets from the trust. For many, an attractive benefit of a trust is that trust assets can avoid probate processes—a local court oversees the distribution of your assets after you pass away. Probate processes are public, and they can sometimes take a lot of time and expense, money that would otherwise pass directly to your loved ones. By creating a trust, you can streamline the process of passing your property directly to your beneficiaries. Some trusts are also able to avoid estate taxes, which can be helpful or useful for people with a lot of assets.

# Insurance

Insurance is another key piece of asset protection. You need good property insurance—not only for you personally but also for your rental properties and business. There are several different factors that I look at when determining what exactly I need.

When it comes to insurance, I always want to make sure I have enough coverage to handle things like a fire or a tree falling on the property. Insurance companies usually offer a cash-value policy and a replacement-cost policy for rental properties. A cash-value policy is usually written for properties that might need a little bit of work done, and the insurance company would pay out in the event of a loss being incurred based on a cash value and what they feel like it would be worth at that particular time, for whatever part of the property was affected.

For instance, if you have a thirty-year roof on your property and a storm comes through and damages it, you would file an insurance claim. If it is a cash-value policy, the insurance company will only pay you the cash value, which is normally prorated to the value of what a thirty-year roof would be. So you would likely not receive enough money to replace the roof.

Whereas, if you had a replacement-cost policy, then the insurance company would pay out based on replacing the roof. This is far better coverage because the insurance is actually paying to repair *all* the damage instead of only giving you a portion of a payout.

Another thing you need to do before signing an insurance policy is to make sure you have a rental income loss benefit. That way, if anything happens to your rental property that results in you not being able to rent it, the insurance company will pay you lost rent for a set period of time (usually, the time in which they classify it to be reasonably repaired and complete).

Obviously, this is a judgment call in every situation, but with this benefit, you would still be making money, even if the property is closed for repairs, which really helps. In fact, that is a game changer when it comes to the rental business.

Now, there will be a premium difference between a cash-value policy and a replacement-cost policy. A replacement-cost policy is always more, but to me, that is pennies on the dollar in comparison to the amount of insurance coverage that you would have. It is always a good working practice to never cut a corner when it comes to insurance, because I would much rather pay a couple hundred extra dollars and have better coverage than to save a couple hundred dollars and pay thousands out of pocket.

Some of you might be thinking, *Look, this isn't my primary residence. I will be fine with bare-minimum insurance on my rental properties.*

I will say it again: your rentals may not be your primary residence, but they are someone else's.

As I mentioned, I once had one of my properties catch fire, causing thousands of dollars' worth of damage. Thankfully, I had the right insurance in place, had the right amount of coverage in place, and was able to put the property back together and rent it out again within a reasonable amount of time. It didn't cost me anything but a deductible. If I had cut corners and just gotten the bare minimum, which would have been just enough to cover my loan on the property, I would probably still be paying for the repair years later.

It took the full amount of coverage to put that particular property back together. The insurance worked well; it took close to a year to turn the property. I was paid a year's worth of lost rent, and the insurance paid to have the property put back together the way it was pre-fire. This is how insurance is supposed to protect your assets. If I had ever doubted paying that extra premium each month, that one experience taught me that it was worth every dime.

Talk through these issues with your local insurance agent on a yearly basis to make sure they have the right coverage in place.

General liability insurance—also called, commercial liability insurance, business liability insurance, or a GL policy—helps protect your business and companies from claims filed due to risks that are part of normal business operations. They can get expensive for small businesses that otherwise do not have the resources to cover the liability claims.

For example, did you know that a slip and fall can cost tens of thousands of dollars? And if you are faced with retribution, harm/loss could cost you even more. Without general liability coverage, your business would have to pay these costs out of pocket. Bodily injury can include a tenant slipping and falling.

General liability also covers the following:

- medical expenses for any worker you might have on payroll
- property damage from employee accidents, like breaking a window
- personal injury
- slander

General liability can help pay if your business is a defendant. It can help cover the cost of property damages, claims against your business, medical expenses if someone gets hurt, administrative costs to handle the covered claims, court costs, judgments, and settlements.

GL insurance does *not* cover some of the following:

- commercial auto accidents while driving for work (you would need a commercial auto policy to cover those damages)
- employee injuries or illnesses that occur while working (workers' compensation insurance gives your employees those benefits)
- state-specific issues (check with your carrier or sales rep to see what those may be for your state)

The danger of not having general liability insurance is that you might have to pay for judgments and settlements, legal defenses, court fees, and so on. All of these can be extremely expensive; you would have to pay out of pocket if you do not have the right general liability insurance in place. I strongly recommend you do this *before* you move a tenant in.

Normally, state law does not require you to carry general liability insurance; not having coverage, however, could put your business at financial risk. Again, this is pennies on the dollar compared to the thousands of dollars it could save you down the road.

In addition, I would also recommend getting a commercial umbrella policy to help provide extra coverage. This type of insurance provides an extra layer of liability protection by covering costs that go beyond what your other liability insurance covers. In other words, commercial umbrella insurance complements your other liability coverages by taking over when your other liability coverage limits have been reached. If you do not have an umbrella policy in place and someone sues you for an amount that exceeds your general liability policy, then you'll have to pay out of pocket to make up the difference.

# Why So Much Insurance?

Some of you are just getting started in this business and might be thinking, Look, Steven, I just want a couple of properties. Just some extra income—I don't need all this insurance.

Others may be thinking, I will get all this once I become a mogul and can afford it.

Either way, allow me to caution you: the bigger you get, the more at-risk you are of getting sued.

If you have two properties, you can still be sued, and you need the correct insurance in place because it only takes one hit to sink your business. For example, if you had two properties and the unthinkable happened—a tenant got hurt while staying in your property, and you were sued for $100,000—if you do not have any general liability insurance in place, you could potentially owe that amount to your tenant.

General liability insurance is not that expensive, and you need it for every single property. As you buy property, continue to add each address to your general liability policies so that they are covered. If you do not add them to your general liability insurance, then your general liability will not cover those particular properties...but your umbrella policy might, because the umbrella policy is for the entire company.

# Know Your Policies

It's important to have the right policies and correct coverage, and it's just as important to actually *know* your policies—what's covered, how much, and even what's *not* covered. If you file a claim and keep good records, then the only way insurance will work to your benefit is by knowing these answers. It is so important to know what coverage you have on the property so you know that information before you actually need it. Remember in the other chapters when I talked about when things go wrong, your emotions are high? You want to know this information *before* your emotions get high, because that can make a world of difference. Study your insurance policies when you have a clear head so you will know what is covered and the amount of coverage.

As a reminder, if you are reviewing your policies each year, you can make changes to your coverage before you actually need it. You will also know when and how to file a claim, and when you should *not* file a claim.

I promise these won't be fun reads, but it is still something that you need to do. Remember back in Chapter Six when we talked about why insurance doesn't cover maintenance and minor repairs? If I have a leaking faucet that does not cause damage to anything, for example, then that is not something that my insurance company will cover. Nor will it cover it due to neglect on my part. I would just need to fix the faucet on my own. But if that faucet was leaking due to a tenant damaging it, and it caused damage to the cabinets, subfloor, or regular flooring, then that is something that you would want to file a claim to recover.

That said, every policy will be a little different, so you need to make sure you know what your policy says in order to determine what they will cover. Make sure you have a great insurance agent because they will help with this process. Insurance agents are paid by having you as a customer, and it is their job to answer any questions and make sure you understand your coverage.

Earlier in the book, we talked about why it's critical to keep good records, and keeping up with your insurance policies' location is no exception. I recommend putting them in a fireproof and waterproof safe or filing cabinet. That way, if and when the time comes that you need to refer to them, and your adrenaline and blood pressure are pumping with urgency, you don't have to add a stressful, frantic search for your policies—you already know where they are kept.

For example, say a storm blows through and tears shingles off of a roof and you have a roof leak; if you already know the amount of coverage that you have and what is covered in your policy, you can go ahead and file your insurance claim either directly with the insurance company or through your insurance agent. This may be helpful, particularly if you get a jump on other claims that other homeowners will file due to the same storm.

# Be Your Own Advocate

Insurance companies will not advocate for you—you have to do that yourself, by way of extra protections like trusts and LLCs.

You have to be your own advocate because insurance companies are not your friends. While I really like my agent, Lance, and consider *him* a friend, he has no control over my insurance company's underwriters.

An insurance company's job is to insure your property, and they are charging you a premium to do that. Their job is to pay out if a covered asset is damaged, but they will not go above and beyond what's outlined in the policy to help you with any of that. Remember, the insurance company is a business; the less money that they pay out is more money that they make.

With that in mind, you have to advocate for yourself and know the information. When you contact a claims adjuster at an insurance company, sometimes they might be new or sometimes they might be seasoned, but if you know your policy, you can help advocate for yourself. Familiarize yourself with your policies; I can't tell you how many times I have had to dig in my heels with claims adjusters and insurance companies because I knew my policy better than they did...and thankfully, my heel-digging led them to pay the way they were supposed to. I could not get preoccupied with offending them when they were telling me things that were not accurate about my own policies. I was able to correct them in real time; I had my policy open and could refer them to specific clauses and paragraphs; and at the end of the day, I had a positive outcome.

Remember my story about the time a tenant sued me personally? The judge dismissed the case because the tenant should have sued the LLC that owned the property. I put the right things in place, in advance. Had I not done that and carried that information with me that day, the case would have been heard; the judge wouldn't have known, nor had access to, that information.

Even if they had sued the LLC, I still would have won, but it would've been a lot more time and expense. The court would have heard the case and would have needed the same sorts of documentation to support my defense—the lease, itemized invoices, copies of communication, and so on. I would've presented these and explained all that to the judge, along with other supporting factors, like "before" and "after" photos. I would have still won because I had all of that in place. I knew that the LLC was the legal owner of the property, and I spent pennies instead of dollars because I had the protections already set up.

You don't always have to become an expert in everything when it comes to business, but you do need to know the basics about how to proactively protect yourself. When it comes to these things, like being sued or anything else that has to do with money, those kinds of situations bring out the worst in people. No one is going to have your back more than you.

Being your own advocate and putting things in place will save you money, but building the right relationships with local agencies and cities can also save you money. In the next chapter, we'll dive into how to protect yourself by understanding local ordinances and codes, and making sure you understand how they work.

# Chapter 9
# Get Familiar with the Locals

When it comes to dealing with the locals in a community you are not very familiar with, you always want to get things in writing because unfortunately, someone's word no longer means what it used to. I learned this the hard way dealing with a local city government.

Anytime I buy a property, I always do due diligence before buying it. This specific property, however, was being rented by the bedroom; in other words, tenants rented rooms, not the entire dwelling. As I mentioned, I did my due diligence before buying it; I contacted the city in which this property was located, and spoke with the correct contacts for my various questions. During that time, I trusted the local city agency that their word actually meant something. As time went on, leadership and management changed, as did the entire city. I mean, it completely changed.

With new management in place, I was told the property could no longer be used in its current capacity. The city was aware of its use the entire time, it was well documented, and I managed the property responsibly, giving them no reason to make any abrupt changes. The city did not care about that, however, and now wanted me to shut it down.

I had to make a decision. Was I going to just comply with what the city wanted me to do now, or should I defend myself and my tenants with evidence that supported my position?

## Rubber, Meet Road

The moral of the story is that you want to be proactive about learning city ordinances and the agencies responsible for them. In addition, you especially want to know what is in place to protect landlords and tenants.

Looking back on that particular incident, I did almost everything right. The two mistakes that I made: one, not getting things in writing, and two, assuming that people would do the right thing and honor their word.

Before purchasing an investment property, make sure that you have all the information that you need in writing. If you own property in a city different from your own, you are responsible for keeping up with local ordinances to better protect yourself long term. Just like we discussed in the previous chapter, you have to be your own advocate...because nobody will advocate for you. City governments are supposed to do the right things for the community, but there are city governments out there that will not, and only care about their own agendas.

# Aren't They Supposed to Help?

Most people think local laws and agencies are there to help. Most of the time, they are, but then there are instances just like mine, where the outcome isn't favorable, and you can't always predict the reasons why. Sometimes, it's just a power struggle; other times, they need to set a precedent. I had done my due diligence, talked to the right people, and thought I did everything right; but years later, it came back to bite me. The laws and ordinances that are in place simply did not work for me in this situation.

Most of the time, local ordinances do not have a ton of gray area within them, but when they do, it is usually up to local agencies—whether that's in a city, town, or consolidated district—to interpret what those gray areas would mean. If you are trying to do something that no longer aligns with what the city wants or their agenda, then they have the power to not allow you to do something or shut you down altogether. In my case, that's exactly what they tried to do.

Regardless, you still need to seek this information directly from the sources. Don't just ask your friend who is also in the rental business; people want to help, but they don't always know everything. You just can't always take someone's word for it. And frankly, you are an outsider to the local community, so I recommend you seek multiple sources in your due diligence. In my own situation, I learned that just because a city tells you something that you can or cannot do, it does not mean they are telling you the truth. Local government is supposed to do what is best for the community; this house was being rented out by the bedroom, which was what the community needed, but the city did not offer me any viable solutions for it. All they cared about was shutting it down because it didn't align with their agenda. Had I taken their word for it, they would have successfully shut it down, but they didn't understand who they were picking a fight with. I had enough experience to know where I could find the correct resources to make a better decision.

What I found out was that the city was not giving me all the options that they should have. By doing my own research, reviewing the ordinances myself, and partnering with a great law firm, I was in a better position to fight this.

Some local governments do have to answer to the state. This was the case for me, living in North Carolina. The state has an agency in place called the Department of Insurance, which gave me guidance on key items that ultimately played a huge role in the favorable outcome I finally received. Cities do use the Department of Insurance to help interpret local codes and ordinances; when I initially contacted them, I didn't think things would necessarily change, but what I did find out was that the city agencies were off base. Had I not contacted them to confirm or refute what the city agency was telling me, then I would not have gotten the outcome that I wanted.

Remember, you have to be your own advocate and fight for what you believe is true and what you believe is right.

Earlier, I mentioned a law firm I hired to help me with my case. They were not local to the area. In my experience, if you use a law firm within the city in which you own rental property, then you might not get some of the outcomes that you are looking for. In my case, most of the law firms that are within the city are also friends with local city officials. So if you use a law firm that is local to the city in which you own property, sometimes those lawyers may have a vested interest to not work as hard for you, because they have more established relationships with individuals at local city offices. An attorney who is not local (but obviously, licensed to practice in that jurisdiction) will be less likely to operate this way; they are there to do a job, and to represent you in the best possible way.

This is not to suggest that someone is unethical or doing something that violates their license; we all have biases, however, and the inclination might be to work on your case with a little more relaxed approach.

I learned this lesson the hard way. When I first fought this particular case, I had hired a local attorney, and I was not getting the results that I wanted. That attorney wanted to be more political about it because he was friends with local officials. After letting him go, I hired an attorney from out of town, one who knew the ordinances in and out, was the expert in the room, and didn't care about making friends. I got the results that I wanted.

Now there are some general aspects of local ordinances, codes, and procedures that you should already know before you get into this business. Ignorance of the law isn't an acceptable defense, trust me. You want to protect yourself, your business, and your tenants.

- Know what the requirements are for building, whether you're installing a fence or preparing a property for short-term rental. Many of these require various permits, inspections, and the like.
- Make sure you dot your i's and cross your t's when it comes to knowing what you can and cannot do in local cities. For example, most cities and towns have codes for minimum housing standards and high grass (the latter being part of what's known as "nuisance ordinances").
- Understand the codes regarding minimum housing standards.
- Find out if there is any sort of overlay on the block where you are looking to purchase.

# Build Solid Relationships

This doesn't mean that good relationships with agencies outside of your local sphere of influence are not possible; you should pursue and maintain good relationships, always, but understand that if you are faced with doing the right thing versus "going along to get along," those relationships may hit a speed bump or two. Sometimes, the right answer is not always popular, but if you maintain good relationships, you will develop a reputation for being a person of character and integrity. There's no positive outcome if you approach these relationships already on the defensive, or think good relationships are not possible; do what you can to forge good rapport, but understand that there may come a time when lines are drawn, and you may find yourself on the opposite side for doing what's right instead of what's popular. It's easier to work with people when you have mutual respect, because when gray areas arise, they have the power to make your life pleasant or unpleasant.

We spent a lot of time in Chapter Three talking about the difference between authentic relationships and using people for personal gain. When we talk about building relationships with city officials, the rules are the same. Be proactive and create authentic relationships before you may actually need that person for something. Understand that the most solid relationships are built over time, not overnight.

For example, if you have a good relationship with a local code enforcement officer who handles the nuisance ordinance for a particular town—and you've already established a good relationship with that person and they know you always do what you say you're going to do—then that person is more apt to call you and tell you to mow your yard if the grass on your rental looks high. I have found that forging those relationships makes things so much smoother because there is mutual respect; you both understand that each person has a job to do, and it won't ever turn personal.

This also means that you maintain a healthy respect for the codes and laws that are in place and do not skate on gray areas; instead, educate the local officials on what you are trying to do in your rental business and what you are facing. Over time, I have educated local code enforcement officers with what we are facing as landlords on a daily basis, and now they understand our side and how things affect us—not just the side of a tenant calling in to complain about a house they claim does not meet minimum housing standards.

In one particular incident, I showed the code enforcement officer photographs of the house before the tenant moved in so they'd understand that I was not moving someone into a house that did not meet minimum housing standards, and that the tenant was actually the one who damaged the home. That built credibility for me when dealing with these same officials on other matters. If you ever have questions regarding inspections, zoning, or anything city-related, give them a call and ask questions up front—that also builds credibility and shows them you are trying to do things the right way.

One more time: *these relationships don't happen overnight.* And sometimes, you have to clean up on the back end instead of building on the front end. One city tried to shut down one of my properties, and it has taken me years since then to forge good relationships on the back end instead of doing it on the front end. The mutual respect had been lost, and they did not understand my position. It is much better and easier to build those relationships up front, even if it takes years to do so; continue to reach out to your local towns and cities to ask questions about certain things. You can explain that you are new to the business, and a new property owner in the area, and you just want to introduce yourself. Let them know that your goal is to provide good, affordable housing, which is always a benefit to any town.

Relationship ROI (return on investment) is key to being successful in this business. This applies to all relationships—city officials, vendors, tenants, lenders, other real estate investors, even your personal friends and family. I would not have what I have today if I did not forge great relationships. People are more apt to help you out if you are respectful and genuine, you care about their position, and you care about them as a human being.

# Trust, but Verify Here, Too

Now when it comes to verifying the information that you are given by local officials, always ask them to cite where they are getting it from. That way, you can verify that they are giving you the correct information.

For example, if you are seeking information on a zoning matter, and you speak to the zoning officer within one of these local agencies, ask them to give you the citation where they are pulling their decision from. Even if you don't think what they are telling you is correct, don't let them know that; instead, take the information that they are giving you, and do your own research to confirm or deny what they are stating is correct. Don't assume anything, especially if you were not provided the right information. People make mistakes—we all do. Staying nonconfrontational will ultimately yield you a better relationship with this individual; waiting to verify a piece of information shows that you are not intentionally picking at someone or seeking to disagree with them.

You are also showing that person respect. It's perfectly fine to verify, because that is what they do before they give you information, including the citation. If the zoning officer does not have a citation to give you, just respectfully ask for it, and let them know that you need it, because you want to make sure you educate yourself to be the best landlord you can possibly be. If you take that approach, you should have better results.

Earlier in the book, I cautioned you against partnerships, and I still believe that partnerships in business are very difficult. While I still do not recommend having a partnership in business with someone, except in very rare circumstances, partnerships with local agencies are a must in this business. I have properties throughout North Carolina, and if I did not have partnerships with different local towns, cities, and counties, then this would have been very difficult to accomplish, much less accomplish successfully. It might not be a great idea to create a partnership in a business deal with someone; however, partnerships are a great idea when it comes to creating relationships with local agencies.

# Zoning, Permits, Codes, and Ordinances

There are four items that you need to have working knowledge of in any given local area: zoning, permits, codes, and ordinances. Every town has zoning requirements, such as a zoning map, that tells you where businesses can be located, where single-family homes and multifamily homes can be located, and so on. When you are buying properties, you need to confirm that your intended use for the property aligns with the zoning.

When it comes to permits, you need to know the basics of what kind of permit is needed, when you need it, and when you don't. Most of your HVAC, electrical, roof, plumbing, and additions will all need permits. You usually do not need permits to paint a house, but double-check whether a permit is required for minor cosmetic repairs just the same. You might need a general renovation permit. These will vary from city to city, county to county. Believe it or not, there is a permit that is supposed to be pulled when you are having a roof replaced, because most cities want to know where your roofer will dump the shingles.

No matter a town's size, I can assure you that when it comes to codes, there will be an entire book of them. You don't need to be an expert on everything, but there are a few basics that you'll need to know, and you'll want to know how to navigate what you don't know (like finding the right people in the Code Enforcement Department and other agencies who usually handle different aspects of various codes). At this stage, all you are looking for is basic code knowledge. For example, if you were putting on a new deck on a house, there are codes for a new deck and certain requirements that need to be met. You would want to pull the code for whatever project you were doing. A lot of code requirements will be inspected if you pull a permit, and most of the permitted jobs have to be completed by a licensed contractor.

Also, there are new codes and old codes; most of the time, you would want the code section based on the version of when your house was last built or updated. For example, if your house was built in the 1980s, you would adhere to the code requirements for the 1980s. But if you are doing renovations, then the city might require you to adhere to the new code.

Ordinances get into the weeds, sometimes literally. For example, most towns have a high-grass ordinance, where your grass cannot grow over twelve inches tall. A lot of cities have ordinances regarding junk cars on the property and leash laws for pets. Some ordinances issue a fine if you are cited multiple times within a year. This is one of those things that you need to know and comply with, because this will affect you more than other items. Ordinances can get rather complicated, but I would certainly consult with the professionals to ensure you are up to speed, and where to go to find out more.

Most local ordinances boil down to items included in minimum housing requirements and nuisance ordinances. Most of the items covered in nuisance ordinances will not require a permit to fix, but they will still need attention. You are still responsible for compliance.

# Never Stray from Doing What's Right

At the beginning of this chapter, I was telling you a story about a property that rented by the bedroom, not by individual dwelling. That was a tough situation, but I was brought up to always do what is right, not what is easy. Once I found out that the city was not forthcoming with all the information and they were not giving me all the options that I was entitled to, I fought back. Fighting back sometimes will not be popular; but I was brought up to do what is right, not what is popular. At the end of the day, the outcome doesn't matter as much as being able to sleep at night, knowing that you did what was right instead of just going along to get along.

In my case, I did what was right. It was years' worth of fighting with this city. It was stressful, but at the end of the day, I did it because not doing it would have created a worse outcome. I would not have been able to sleep at night, knowing I did not do everything I should have done, because it was going to affect so many people. The individuals who lived at this property did not have a voice, and I had to be the voice for them. The property is called something different now, but it is still able to operate—just under different terms.

Had I not advocated for myself and those individuals to try to find a solution, then I would not have gotten the same outcome. Thankfully, I had existing relationships with key agencies, but they were strained a bit during this period. I have been diligent to heal and repair what I can, and continue to conduct business there in the same respectful manner that I always have. Most, if not all, of those relationships have been restored.

Sometimes, you have to do unpopular things because it is the right thing to do. In this case, I fought for the people. We got the outcome that we wanted, where people were allowed to continue renting out bedrooms. This kept many of them off the streets, which ultimately benefits the city, too. It is a win-win, though it was still a challenging time. A city should never be against its taxpayers; it is supposed to be a partnership that makes a better community in which we live.

With this in mind, you always want to do the right thing, and part of that means educating yourself on what the right thing might be. Never assume that you know everything, because you don't. In the next chapter, I will talk more about how you continue to learn throughout this business as you grow.

# Chapter 10
# Continuing Education: You Don't Know It All

Stay ahead of the plane.

I learned this phrase when I studied to get my pilot's license. What it means is that you always want to stay ahead of what might be coming. For example, the weather forecast, not just from your take-off location but also where you're landing. Or your fuel levels and instruments—you always want to stay ahead to detect anything that might go wrong.

This phrase applies in the rental business and in life, too: *stay ahead.*

How do we do this in the rental business, or any business?

Look, I'm going to level with you: you do not know everything, and neither do I.

None of us can predict the future, but we can study, learn from history, and become an expert on things to help us have better outcomes in life and in business. Continue to educate yourself on the business of rental properties. Follow real estate trends, for example—is the market going up, or down? Do you have enough savings? Do you have enough emergency money for the rainy day? All of these things are extremely important in being successful in business where you might not be able to predict the future, but you can do certain things along the way to help your future be more successful.

The more open you remain to learning, the better success you'll have. I have been in this business for many years, and I still don't know everything. If I had that mindset that I knew everything, and didn't remain open to new ideas, then I wouldn't have enjoyed nearly as much of the successes that I have today. A few examples:

- I would not have loaned money.

- I would not have flipped houses.
- I would not have diversified my investments and would've instead kept all my eggs in one basket.
- I would not have started a consulting business.
- I would not have written this book.

It is so important to keep an open mind about learning, not only in business, but in life. When you surround yourself with people who have more experience than you do, you will learn far more and become more successful than if you don't. Not surprisingly, if you think you know everything, then you will have a closed-minded outlook, which will not allow you to reach your full potential.

Experience cannot be bought. It is something that you just have to learn over time. So make sure that you use other people's experiences—whether they're successes or failures—and make sure to learn from them.

In fact, some of the best learning opportunities in life are from failures. Accept that you will make some missteps, especially in the beginning of your real estate career. When you experience a failure, that is actually a starting point for your net success! You want to learn from your failures so you don't have to relearn over and over again; when you fail, that's a great starting point for your next opportunity, whatever it may be, and you can redirect what you're actually trying to accomplish.

If you think about it, what better starting point is there than to emerge from a failure? Some of the greatest blessings in my own life have come from failures. You don't know how good you have it if you have no failures to compare.

# Rates, Rentals, Financing, Trends

Right now, you might be thinking, *Why should I keep learning about rates, rentals, financing, and trends?* And you may have already enjoyed some success in the rental arena, so it's easy to think, *I've got this.* But that is short-lived because all of it changes over time. I constantly look at all four of these items on a monthly basis because these four things have a lot to do with whether I will be successful or not. You want to remain in a state of learning—learn new ways to navigate this business. By studying these four items, over time, you will better predict what the market potentially might do.

For example, I'm always looking at what rental rates will be, because I want to make sure my rents are in line with comparable properties in the area. By keeping your rental rates within the range of the going rate, you will keep your properties full long term.

I also keep a close eye on rates, financing, and current market trends. Usually, I look at all three of these together. I have never been one to focus much on interest rates, because my renters are the ones making the monthly payments for me, and I am using someone else's money to buy the property. Interest rates don't mean as much to me, as long as the property cash flows correctly. But it is important to know what the market rates are doing for your financing options, and what your interest rates are, because you are evaluating a property based on the current market for that day. If it's good today and rates go through the roof, then the market turns into a bad market, and you might not make any money.

Keep this on repeat: be conservative when you evaluate. And when you evaluate what mortgage rates are doing, along with the financing options you have available, and what the markets are doing, then you can provide yourself with an educated analysis of what you think the market is going to do in the future. For instance, you might be able to predict whether interest rates, market prices, and home values are going up or down. I will caution you a little on this method because many people did not see the housing crisis coming in the late 2000s. So this is not going to be an exact science, but it does give you a good, well-educated guess about what you feel like the market's going to do.

# Finding New Solutions to Old Problems

When you stay open-minded and humble, you put yourself in a better position to learn. Earlier, I mentioned that this mindset led me to flipping houses and lending money.

My business has always been buying and holding rental properties, but I wanted to learn a different income stream. We were coming out of the COVID pandemic, and I realized that it is very hard to be successful with just one revenue stream. So even though I knew quite a bit about rental properties and how to fix them up in preparation for a renter, I did not have a ton of experience when it came to buying properties, fixing them up, and actually selling them to an individual. These are two completely different things.

Instead of going in with a mindset of thinking I know how to buy properties and I know how to fix up properties, i.e., "anybody can do this," I recognized that I needed to learn from someone who had more experience with actually flipping houses. I let them guide me to make sure that I did everything the right way. Had I not done that, then I would not have had as much success in flipping houses, which has now become a very successful part of my business.

I had also never considered financing properties. Essentially, I act as the bank, loaning people money to buy real estate. This is done in two different ways: seller financing and buyer financing. Since I had little experience on how this was done, I leaned on people who knew more about how to do this correctly.

In both of these situations and in others, I have learned to seek out those who had more experience than me. Had I not been a good student—open to new things and respectful of what my "teacher" knew—I would not have been successful in these new ventures. I learned the mistakes to avoid, and I did not make the same mistakes that they did. That is valuable advice!

Stay open to learning from someone who has more experience; find a mentor who can give you the right information. This has made a tremendous difference in how I do business, and even the types of businesses I handle. In both areas, they are now key players in my overall business dealings because they have been successful ventures. That's what happens when you understand that you might not know everything, and you surround yourself with great people who have been there before you—because experience is priceless.

# Predict the Curve

Once you can apply an educated guess on what you feel like the market is going to do, you can make sound adjustments to your rental rates, property prices, and even their value. You can make better decisions regarding the way you might fix up a property to how you might collect rent.

When you can predict the curve, you can stay ahead. Some aspects are going to be a lot easier to predict than others, but there are many resources you can consult and refer to—bankers, Realtors, and the good ol' internet— that can provide you with data, analyses, and trends that will help you run your business more efficiently. There is not a one-size-fits-all solution for us. It's up to you to put all of it together and make it work for the common good of your business.

For me, I look at current rental rates and various financial rates— mortgage rates, property values, what a given property could sell for—and determine whether it is still good for me to buy or sell in that market, depending on what I am considering. Then, I take it a step further, looking to see what that property might be worth in the future. Remember, you are not just buying a property for today; you are buying it for the next ten to twenty years. Many people use rental property to fund their retirement, which could be the right answer for you.

You can also predict the curve of your business operations. Over the years, how people find and rent properties has changed significantly. Many prospective tenants opt for virtual tours of a property, for example, and tenants may pay through a tenant portal. Those are trends that you want to evaluate on a regular basis; this keeps you in the position to be proactive instead of reactive. You will almost always make better decisions when you are in a proactive mindset rather than a reactive one.

During the pandemic, someone gave me the idea to look into lending money as a different revenue stream. Initially, I thought it could be a great idea, but I knew nothing about it. So I had some fear about this unknown, since this would be a brand-new venture for me. They walked me through the dos and don'ts to make sure I sidestepped some of their own mistakes. I learned that a lot of it came down to how you structure a deal—the length of the loan, down payments, monthly payments, and so on. Today, this has become a large portion of my business. Staying open and "remaining teachable" opened up a brand-new way to make money, which allowed me to diversify my investments and mitigate risk.

# Hidden Gems

Back in Chapter 1, we covered quite a bit of ground about what to look for in a mentor. I always tell people to be cautious about taking advice from flashy people because they might not be as genuine as they may seem. One of my go-tos for advice is a gentleman who was wildly successful...yet he drove a normal vehicle, wore normal clothes, and was just an ordinary guy. Yes, he owned a very nice beach house, but he did not leverage those things to get people to "buy into" his program or philosophy.

As someone who prefers to move in silence and allow results to speak for themselves, I am leery of those who seem to spend a lot of time posting the alleged spoils of their success—cars, planes, beachfront homes, etc. So many of those items can be rented by the hour; a few hours and a photo shoot later, these individuals try to convince others to buy into a formula for success that isn't real. Some may be telling the truth, but it is difficult to discern unless you know them personally.

Now admittedly, I am moving a bit more into the spotlight as I launch a consulting business. My intention there, however, is the same intention as those who have helped me—it's time for me to reach back, help others who are trying to break into this business, and let them learn from my own experiences, good and bad. There is a huge difference between someone who is genuine and authentic and someone who is being flashy. You want to surround yourself with people who actually care about you and want to help you be successful.

No, having nice things isn't bad or evil. In fact, nice things can be a lot of fun! Just understand that there is a difference between someone being flashy and someone being authentic. Most of the time, the people that will help you out the most are the ones who are the hidden gems. They are the best educators in this business.

My mentor was not posting on social media about money that he had. He was just an ordinary guy trying to provide for his family and was very successful at it. Those hidden gems are not going to be the ones that you find at every turn; they are hidden for a reason. They are not spending a bunch of time on social media posting about their success. Good mentors don't always advertise on a daily basis that they would be a good mentor, but those are the ones that you need to find!

I launched SOARX Consulting, my consulting and coaching business, for this very reason. I want to provide an authentic step-by-step process on how to do this business, for anyone interested in leveling up in life. I know what it's like to be making $45,000 a year and carrying $75,000 in debt; I also know what it's like to be in the top "1 percent." I make sure that I am providing all the information and that no steps are left out. I'm ready to be a resource and mentor to ensure each client has the tools they need to be successful. I want to demonstrate best practices for social media, using it as a tool that helps instead of just being "flashy for flash's sake."

Admittedly, SOARX Consulting is taking me a bit out of my comfort zone, too. I'm used to quietly going about my business, moving in silence, and letting the results speak for themselves. Launching SOARX is a healthy path for me to take, because it will grow and stretch me to be "out there," while allowing me the opportunity to demonstrate that there is a right way to navigate this business and to help people realize that real estate investing doesn't just have to be a pipe dream.

# True Wisdom Is Priceless

I will say it again: you don't know everything, and neither do I.

Surround yourself with people who have come before you, because they have a lot more experiences and reputable insight than you do. When you do that—and allow yourself to be teachable—you have unlocked true wisdom and placed yourself in a good position to be successful.

Remember, you don't always have to be the smartest person in the room. It's okay just to be an average person wanting to do business, because that's who I was—and deep down, still am—and I just surround myself with people who are far more experienced. There will always be someone who has walked your path before, and they can lead you down the right road.

Knowledge and wisdom alone won't get you there, however; you actually have to put in the hard work to get you where you want to go. I had been working so hard to purchase and manage rental properties; it hadn't occurred to me that I needed to diversify my business interests…and then the pandemic hit. While our tenants were able to take advantage of the assistance that was offered and we did not suffer as badly as other rental businesses, it occurred to me that in order to mitigate risk, I needed to create new and different revenue streams to help offset any sudden blows like that. By staying open and willing to learn, I built successful ventures in flipping houses, lending money, and other investments, in a relatively short period of time. In the next chapter, I'll dive deeper into why diversifying your investments is such a big deal.

# Chapter 11
# Diversify Your Investments

There is an old saying that my parents always told me: "Don't put all your eggs in one basket."

To continue where we left off in the last chapter, I had to pivot quickly during the COVID pandemic. Most of my income was from rental income, where tenants paid monthly. But during the pandemic, the government issued a moratorium on eviction of tenants for nonpayment of rent. Essentially, tenants could decide whether they wanted to pay rent or not—not a great situation for any landlord to be in! Fortunately, most of my tenants paid their rent because we worked extremely hard to get them the help they needed to make those payments.

This certainly got me thinking about what-ifs. What if I had not been able to convince my tenants to apply for rental assistance? What if they had shrugged and said, "Oh well. You can't throw us out either way"?

Let me shift gears here and say that this is another reason you want good relationships, even with your tenants. Had I been one of those landlords who was not responsive or did not keep up the properties, they could have easily not lifted a finger to help me. Then, I wouldn't have made the income I made, and my business might not have survived during that two-year period.

In the meantime, as I thought about all the what-ifs, that saying floated to the surface: *Don't put all your eggs in one basket.*

"Have you ever considered loaning money to people?" a Realtor friend asked me one day.

"What do you mean?" I asked. After all, I was already grateful for the income that was coming in, but by no means was I comfortable—I was watching every dime just in case. So loaning money? Where was she going with this?

"I mean loaning money as a secondary income," she replied. Now I was intrigued. To me, loaning money meant never expecting to get it back. How does that create income?

She walked me through how it works, how to structure it, and what makes someone a "good" risk. When I spoke with others who were doing this, I sought even more advice, and of course, I did my due diligence so that I would have a good idea as to whether this was a good fit for me.

Eventually, I took the leap. Loaning money provided me with a good secondary income, since my primary income was not as strong as what it was pre-pandemic.

# Diversify Now, Not Later

No one could have predicted what happened in 2020; I had to think really quickly about diversifying my investments, because one income stream may dwindle or be shut down completely. Never in a million years did I think our government would allow tenants to go several years without paying rent.

When it comes to diversifying your revenue streams, you want to prepare for the unthinkable. Having those tools in place, along with staying open to learning something new, allowed me to pivot quickly when other businesses went under. Knowing how to research, and putting that research through the lens of my current business practices, enabled me to determine what made the most sense for me. This helped me stay ahead, stay proactive, and continue to advocate for myself instead of being in a position to "beg," so to speak. Diversifying my business interests ensures that if one portion of my business is struggling, the whole business will not suffer.

# Make Money While You Sleep

Rental properties continue to be the main source of revenue for my business, but I quickly learned that there are fields of opportunities that generate more revenue streams, including house-flipping, financing properties, compound interest investments, and so on. This helps balance the highs and the lows.

Now I am prepared, in case the unthinkable happens again, or if one part of my business is underperforming. For example, there could come a time when I have tenants that do not pay, and I have to evict a lot of people—and evictions cost money. Or maybe there will be a period where I just can't find a good deal for me to buy and flip for a good profit. Perhaps there will be an instance where I finance a property for someone and they don't pay, and I have to foreclose on them. If one piece is struggling, it won't all struggle at the same time.

When asked, I always advise people getting into this business to make money while you sleep. Make sure that, however you choose to diversify, all your investments are making you more money, not less. There is only so much time in the day, and time is one thing that you cannot buy more of. Make sure you are working smarter, not harder, for your money.

I have heard it suggested that most millionaires have seven different income streams—and most millionaires that I know have quite a few revenue streams, though I've never stopped to count exactly how many. For me, that would include rental property income, flipping houses, financing properties, investments (including compound interest investments), speaking engagements, consulting, and houses that appreciate over time. Now that last one, in full transparency, does not make money right away but would definitely generate quite a bit when I sell it. These are seven that I focus on, but there are so many other ways to create seven different types of revenue that are not just limited to real estate. There is no right or wrong answer when it comes to that; you just have to decide for yourself what makes the most sense.

If you are thinking about getting into real estate, it can be a very nervous and fearful time. Any new venture that creates a new revenue stream could bring a little fear along with it; that is just a natural way of thinking about the unknown. It is perfectly human to be fearful when you don't know what the next steps are. I was the same way when I got into the rental business, when I got into the house-flipping business, and when I got into the business of loaning money. In fact, it's fair to say I have a bit of hesitation each time I embark on something new, because there is an unknown factor to it. This is to be expected, and should only pause you long enough to be sure you are covering as many bases as you can, acknowledging that you cannot predict the future, and giving yourself grace for any missteps along the way.

I alleviate a lot of fear by continuing to educate myself to make sure I am doing the right thing and surrounding myself with people who have far more experience than I do. Having someone to help guide you and knowing where to find information to help guide you along the way will give you the confidence you need to take the next step.

And be sure to celebrate each step. You bought this book to learn more about real estate investing—that is a big first step, and congratulations to you for having done so. Finding a mentor is another milestone to celebrate; solid coaching will move mountains in this business. Conducting research and educating yourself is another celebratory step—you are learning new things, including how to filter and distill what is integral to move you forward. You are getting tools that you need, just like you have with buying this book—continue gathering the tools that you need to be successful. In fact, one of the reasons I created SOARX is to help people get where they want to be, and sincerely celebrate their successes. I created a course that takes clients through this business, step by step.

# Flip or Rent?

Some of you may be wondering how flipping houses produces income. After all, you're putting money into a house, and it's not really income if you're putting money into something...right?

Flipping houses produces a revenue stream immediately after you sell the property, whereas investment properties and rental properties produce income over time. I tend to lean a bit more toward long-term investments, because I want to make more money long term, but it was important for me to balance that with money that can be made in the short term. This is where flipping houses comes into play.

This is a unique revenue stream because you can buy property at a decent price, put money into the property, and then sell it for a profit. On the flip side of that, however, you have to be very careful because you could pour a lot of money into it and not make a dime. You make your money on the buy; if you overpay for a house, fix it up, and sell it, the selling price is going to be the same, no matter what you bought the property for.

For example, if you bought a house for $100,000 and put $50,000 into it and sold it for $200,000, you'd make $50,000. But what if you bought the property for $50,000, put $50,000 into it, and sold it for $200,000? Then, you are making $100,000. Always be mindful of the buying price because your selling price might not change. Make sure you are putting yourself in a position to actually generate *more* revenue instead of just pouring more money into something and not making anything extra on it.

Now when determining which houses I'm going to flip versus rent, I do consider certain criteria. It's not an exact science, but I primarily look at how much money I will have tied up in a certain property—the price of the house, the repair costs, average rental rate, and how much money I can make over time if I hold on to it and rent it. Then I compare this with the purchase price, repair costs, and flipping costs (which go beyond actual repairs). At the end of the day, it comes down to the cash flow:

- How much am I going to make in either scenario?
- How many years will it take me to recoup my money renting it versus just flipping it?

Sometimes, it might make more sense to simply flip it, because otherwise I will have too much money tied up in it long term. Flipping it would make me a quicker buck.

To give you an example of how my system works: I currently have a house that I purchased pre-pandemic, originally intending to rent. It's a three-bedroom, one-bath home, and I paid $32,000 for it. At the time, I thought I was only going to need to put $15,000 to $20,000 in it.

Labor prices skyrocketed during COVID. Once I started getting estimates, that $15,000 to $20,000 quickly turned into $60,000 or $70,000. That meant I would have just over $100,000 invested in a rental that I could only rent for $950 to $1,000 per month.

To me, it didn't make sense to hold on to it as a rental. The numbers didn't make sense after the amount of money I would actually clear after payment, taxes, insurance, and upkeep. When I ran the numbers to flip the house, it turned out I could put $70,000 into it and list it for $240,000. That made more sense; I could make $140,000 at one time, whereas renting it would take me fifteen years to make that same amount.

# Compound Interest Funds

Compound interest is interest that you earn on top of interest. For example, if you have $1,000 in an account and it pays 1 percent annual interest, you will earn ten dollars in interest after one year in compounded interest. Year two, you will earn 1 percent interest on $1,010, and the principal will go up by $10.10 in the interest payout for that year.

The best interest investments to take advantage of are *compound* interest investments, which normally yield far more than the 1 percent in the example that I provided.

Certificates of deposit (CDs) are a great example, and largely ignored by many investors. If you are a beginner investor and you want to take advantage of compound interest the right way with little to no risk possible, CDs and savings accounts might be the way to go. CDs normally require minimum deposits but will pay you interest on regular intervals and typically at a higher interest rate than normal savings accounts.

The next would be high-end or high-yield savings accounts. High-yield savings accounts usually require no minimum balance, or very little if they do, and pay a higher interest rate than a normal savings account gives you.

Bonds and bond funds are usually seen as good compound interest investments. They are essentially loans one gives to a creditor, whether that's a company or government, and that entity then agrees to give a specific yield of return for the investor buying the debt.

Money market accounts are interest-bearing accounts similar to CDs. Unlike high-yield savings accounts or CDs, which also pay higher interest rates than traditional savings accounts, money market accounts often allow for paper checks and debit-card privileges. This allows easy access to your assets while earning a higher rate of return.

Stocks and dividend stocks can compound your money even faster. While stocks are a good investment to compound, dividend stocks may be even better. Dividend stocks are a one-two punch, as the underlying assets can keep increasing in value while paying dividends to you.

Finally, real estate investment trusts (REITs) are a great way to diversify your portfolio by investing in real estate without having to buy property outright. There are plenty of REIT investors out there that you can link up with, and I would highly recommend consulting them for more information.

And I would strongly recommend consulting with a fiduciary financial professional to see which one of these routes might work best for you. Fiduciaries have a legal obligation to act in your best interest. When you hire a fiduciary, it may seem like more money up front, but it is actually less money, and they can explain how their fees work.

# Financing Income

What do I mean by "financing income"? I mean that I am financing someone else's dream. I am financing real estate deals for other people, giving them another option besides a bank. I make interest income from those endeavors, as I am acting as a bank in these instances.

For some people, this is a great form of income because you have the property as collateral. If something happens to the property, the insurance pays you as the loss payee to protect the assets you have financed. If the person does not pay, then you can foreclose on the property, get the property back, and keep any payments paid and interest earned, along with the down payment. Then you can turn the property around and finance the property back out, making even more money. This is a great way to diversify and have some alternative income on top of your rental business. I have done this multiple times, and I have made quite a bit of money doing it.

# Soon, but Not All at Once

Your head might be hurting a bit right now; you may be thinking these dreams are far beyond what you can reach. Let me assure you: they are not. I'm living proof.

Remember, I was just a guy working as a retail manager, $75,000 in debt, and I had a dream of getting into the rental business. I have made that dream a reality with success that has exceeded far beyond what I could have ever imagined. If you surround yourself with the right people, work hard, and stay open to new ideas, you could go beyond what I have accomplished, and I would applaud you every step of the way! Yes, there will be sacrifices along the way, but you don't have to be the smartest person in the room or have the most money to achieve and succeed.

The one thing that nobody can take away from you is how hard you work and outwork the next person. Because at the end of the day, working hard is something that you *can* control. You do not have to do everything simultaneously; you do not have to come out of the chute buying rentals, flipping houses, and investing in various entities. These are things I had to add on and build over a period of years. Have the courage to take that leap of faith.

With that being said, as you continue to grow your rental business, you never want to put all your eggs in one basket; you want to continue to diversify your investments so that you can protect yourself against the unthinkable, and protect yourself against something that might go wrong in the general course of business. There will always come a day when something doesn't cash-flow like you thought it was going to, and you need something to help supplement that. Diversify as you can to set yourself up for success.

At the start of the pandemic, I only had one form of investment, and that was rental property. I quickly learned that I needed to diversify, and I spent most of the pandemic setting up new and exciting revenue streams to shore up the gaping hole that COVID had made in my business. I took a leap of faith during a trying time in our country; I am a better business owner, leader, and man coming out of it. My latest venture is the launch of SOARX, a coaching and consulting business that helps others get into the rental business. More on that later.

In the next chapter, we will focus on day-to-day operations to reach your goals because as you diversify, it does create more work. It is important, then, to make sure your day-to-day operations are running smoothly and in line with what your goals are so you can reach those goals.

# Chapter 12
# The Rental Process

I t was my first eviction in the business, and I was lost. I was overwhelmed. I did not want to mess up...but I did not know what kind of paperwork needed to be filled out, and the different timelines that had to be met in order for the eviction to comply with eviction laws. I was nervous. What would the judge say to me if I got something wrong? What would the people in the courtroom think if I messed up? So many things were running through my mind.

Thankfully, I had a network. I surrounded myself with great people who knew far more than I did, and they helped guide me to ensure that I hit every guideline correctly and hit the timelines correctly. By doing this, I had a very successful eviction.

When you are new to the rental business, you will not know everything about the rental process, and everything will seem like it's moving really fast. Many years in, I still don't know everything, so let me assure you that this is a perfectly normal feeling—not just for the rental business but for life in general. Anytime I feel like I do not know the answers to how the rental process works or is supposed to be working—yep, you guessed it—I surround myself with those who know more, and I find answers.

## Know Before You Need: The General Process

From start to finish, the rental process is very complex. When you are in the thick of it, and you're new to the business, it's easy to not know what your next steps should be. This does not get you off the hook, however. You never want to make excuses in this business; ignorance is not bliss. In fact, ignorance can get you into trouble fast. I would highly recommend you educate yourself on the different procedures within the rental process itself. That way, if you don't know a particular process, you will be educated enough to know where to find the information and become an expert on how the process works. The more information you can teach yourself, the better the process will work, and the better landlord you will become. So you don't have to know everything—but you need to know something, and do your best to not overlook anything.

For the most part, the rental process has not changed its core values and core roles, so you're not looking to reinvent the wheel when the wheel is just fine. There is always room for improvement, however. Just make sure you know the general steps so that you don't accidentally eliminate any— you need all of the steps for the whole process to work correctly.

Before you list a property for rent, make sure:

- your rental property company is set up correctly;
- you are protected for the unthinkable; and
- your processes are in place—how you will list the property, take applications, select a tenant, fill out a lease, and move someone in.

After you have your rental company set up and have purchased your first property, you'll want to walk through that property—after repairs and upgrades—and make sure that it is rentable. You may already have a ballpark figure in mind for what you want to rent it for, but now is the time to start thinking about specific numbers.

Next, you'll want to determine the monthly rate and what terms you want to have for the renter, such as the length of a lease and any deposits you'll collect in advance. A rental market rate for your property's current area can be found easily online, and it will differ from market to market. As you consider market-rate rents, keep in mind that you need to compare apples to apples, and not apples to oranges. For instance, you may find market rent is a certain amount for a brand-new property that has all new upgrades, but your property might not be updated. Make allowances for things like this.

From there, you'll start putting together your application and lease processes. Once you have these in place, you will want to put together a game plan for how you want to list the properties—various rental websites, newspapers, or even putting a For Rent sign in the front yard. Once you select a tenant, then you will start filling out your lease paperwork, collecting money, and moving tenants in.

The process does not stop there, because you have to manage the property, and that's ongoing. So you'll need to already have policies in place to make sure that the tenants are paying you on time, according to the lease, and plan for what happens if they don't pay you on time. You'll need to have an eviction process in place and know how you would go about getting your property back if the tenant does not pay. And whether a tenant moves out by election or notice, you'll start all over again. It's a never-ending cycle.

Remember, you want to be proactive, and you do not want to figure out what the steps look like in real time. Know what the processes and steps look like before you actually use them.

Now that you have a bird's-eye view of the rental process, let's unpack some of the finer details—applications, leases, evictions, tenants, tenant payments, rental rates, and what protects landlords and tenants.

# The Listing

What should you include in the listing of your property? You always want to make sure you have good photos of the property's interior and exterior. This will cut down on the number of questions you will get from potential tenants asking what the property might look like. You also want to include the basic information—number of bedrooms and bathrooms, the type of heating and cooling systems, whether rent includes utilities, maintenance, and so on.

If the home has special features and you have room to do so, list them. Does the unit have washer and dryer hookups? Do you allow pets? How will they apply to rent the property? If you have all of this information included, it will streamline your listing and will help reduce the number of questions you receive, plus weed out potential tenants who would not be interested.

How will you advertise your listing? Think about the type of tenant you hope to attract, and research where they are likely to see your listing. I use several different platforms, such as Facebook Marketplace and Realtor.com, or I put a For Rent sign out in the front yard and sometimes take out an ad in the newspaper.

# The Application

Some of the nicest people out there will rob you blind if they have a chance. I don't write that to scare you, just to warn you that you will meet some of the nicest people, they'll tell you the wildest stories, and if you're not careful, they will also not pay rent.

If the specifics outlined in your listing are the first step in your tenant-screening process, then the application is the second. You want to make sure that you have a process in place to take applications and to get the correct information from potential tenants so that you can make the right decision as to whether they are a good fit—and not because they are charming.

I used to do this old-school, where I printed an application, met the prospective tenant in person, showed them the property, and had them complete the application on-site. Now that I have taken my realty management company virtual, I have software that allows people to fill out applications online. There are many different inexpensive software options that allow you to take applications over virtual platforms, and I highly recommend them.

When you review the applications, make sure your standards are all already in place so that you are making objective decisions. Now it is very important to have good standards as a landlord, but they must be ethical, not discriminatory. For example, my standards for tenants include a form of income—a steady job, alimony, or even retirement income—and they must have no evictions on their record for the last three years. They must make three to four times whatever the rent is in income, and provide proof of this. They should have good references, but I also must verify that their references are not their best friend or mother. References must include former landlords. I also have standards for the number of people who are living there. Likely, there are local ordinances that also place a cap based on the number of bedrooms.

By the same token, there are some things that you should not take into consideration when setting standards, including race, gender, and disabilities.

The application should include basic questions ranging from their name and address, previous landlords, employment, and whether they have any eviction or criminal history. You want to make sure that an application is filled out in its entirety.

The next step will be background and credit checks. You do not have to do this for every applicant, only the top two or three applicants, but I do require an application fee that covers both checks. The current software that I use has a $35 fee, which covers both the background and credit checks. Some may charge anywhere from $50 to $65, which covers your background and credit checks, but it'll also cover your administrative fees for processing them all.

These checks are huge, and getting authorization from someone in the application is just as important. Most applications I have used ask for permission to run background and credit checks, but make sure the applicant has signed allowing this. A background check and credit check give you a snapshot of this person's life—the good, the bad, and the ugly. You'll get a clearer picture of whether they pay their bills and what their credit looks like.

Now there is no one-size-fits-all rule when it comes to this, because I have rented to people who have criminal backgrounds, but my biggest deciding factor is whether they have changed their life. So if their arrest was recent and they have charges pending, then that is probably not somebody I would rent to. But if the charges were ten years ago, they have learned from it, and they have not made the same mistake or any other mistake since then, that might be somebody I would rent to.

Similarly, if their credit does not meet all requirements that you would like, but they are doing all the right things because they're trying to build their credit back, then maybe you can make an exception. Read the credit checks, how they are currently making payments, and if they are currently doing the responsible things. That's not to say that we do not take credit scores into consideration, but we handle this on a case-by-case basis.

So now you have selected your tenant, and they need to sign a lease and pay the deposits. I never move someone in without a deposit, and I would highly recommend you do not do this either. At a minimum, I would require a month's worth of rent; depending on the situation and what the background checks and rental history reveal, sometimes I require a double deposit. Again, this is determined on a case-by-case basis, but we do have a standard where we do not allow anyone to move in without paying a deposit.

Your lease and supporting documents are the final piece, and they should come in tandem with the deposits. When it comes to leases and supporting documents, you want to make sure that everything is completed, from their name being filled out correctly to the correct address and correct rental amounts. If one thing is not filled out correctly on the lease, that can hurt you down the road if you ever have to file an eviction or take legal action against your tenant.

Other documents that you always want to make sure are signed include the following:

- the maintenance addendum, which fully outlines what the tenant's responsible for and what the landlord is responsible for
- move-in and move-out inspection reports, verifying the property is in good order
- a lead-based paint addendum, to protect you against someone who might say that they were poisoned from lead-based paint
- pet addendum, if you're going to allow pets (most of the time, I do not allow pets in my rentals for the simple reason that they do so much damage)
- proof of renters insurance

That last bullet point is a huge one. We used to encourage renters insurance, and now we require it from all of our tenants. I would highly recommend that you do not move anyone into a rental unit without renters insurance, because not only does this protect the tenant and their items inside the home that they are renting, but it also adds a layer of protection ensuring that if they tear up anything, you'll be covered under their policy.

Now with that said, all rental policies and rental insurance policies differ a bit, so you would need to consult with each policy directly to make sure you are getting one that covers everything you need covered. The bottom line is that you need to make sure *everyone* is protected.

# The Tough Conversations

Just like any relationship, there will be some tough conversations you need to have with your new tenant, and I strongly recommend that you have them up front. I have learned that, especially in business, if you have honest and transparent conversations up front, then things will go a lot smoother long term. They may not like what they hear initially, but it's much better to go ahead and have that conversation anyway...before a different, even tougher conversation has to happen suddenly.

For example, if you have an applicant who does not meet the "triple the rent" income requirement, and their income is only double the rent, do not wait or string them along. Have that conversation in real time; it will not go as well if the tenant's time has been wasted and they could have spent it looking for rentals they can afford.

Another old saying my parents always taught me: treat others the way you want to be treated. If you were in their shoes, you would want to know the truth up front instead of being strung along.

No matter how strict your standards and countenance are, there will come a prospective tenant who seems so nice...but they have stuff in their application, or the background checks come back with something that doesn't meet your standards. How important are those standards when you encounter somebody who just seems really nice. What do you do?

There is a human element to the rental process, and you are going to feel bad or sorry for certain people in certain situations, and you want to help out as many people as you can. I'm the same way; I get it. Nonetheless, you need to stick to your standards because your standards are going to keep you out of trouble. Just because someone is nice, and just because you might feel for them, this does not pay your bills. I have tried to help others before in this way, and it has backfired every single time. It is unfortunate, but you are running a business, and you need to try to leave the emotions at the door. Make sure that people meet your standards whether they are nice or not.

# Stay Organized

We covered the importance of staying organized earlier, but let me reaffirm that it is an essential part of the rental process. If you do not have a system in place to stay organized, then you will not know where you are in the rental process.

The more organized that you are, the more confidence you will have in carrying out the responsibilities of the rental process. Organization will pay dividends, especially if you are new to the process and new to the business. But even if you are seasoned and several years into this business, well-organized business operations make it very easy to actually...well, *operate*.

For example, I have a filing system organized by property address. Each property has a folder containing a lease for that particular property. That way, if I have a question or if a tenant calls, I know exactly where to look, and I only have to pull one folder instead of having to look through them all. I would encourage you to alphabetize your files by street name instead of numerically by full street address, because as you acquire more properties, that will be a lot of numbers you would have to recall!

You will also need a system to keep up with rents and deposits, because you will be handling these on a monthly basis. I would recommend getting some sort of rental software that helps you manage all of the units. Some are very inexpensive, but regardless, there is one out there that will suit your needs.

This is particularly important to have in place if a tenant falls behind on rent. I charge a 5 percent late fee, and thanks to the software I use, that fee is automatically charged at 5:00 p.m. on the fifth day of each month. My tenants know this because we go over it when they sign the lease. I used to do it the old-fashioned way, and we would call tenants who were late on rent starting on the sixth of the month. Now, I have rental management software that sends out notifications via text or email anytime they are late, and as I mentioned, they are automatically charged this fee in our billing system. I will not waive the 5 percent late fee, because it sets a precedent, and the tenant will do it again. That lease is a legal, binding contract that you not only hold yourself accountable to but also your tenants. Make sure you already have these processes and policies in place and that your tenant is clear on those steps should they fail to pay their rent on time.

# Evictions

If you are already charging late fees, it is essential that you look ahead and make sure you are clear on your eviction process, whether or not you might actually have to file one. This will really come down to what your lease allows, and you must comply with any laws or local ordinances in place.

Keep in mind that you do not want to jump into an eviction just because someone is late paying their rent one time; if that is your eviction policy, then plan on always having vacant properties. While I will still enforce the late fee, this is still very much a human business, and there is no need to go through the red tape required for an eviction if someone is a couple of days late, particularly if they do not have a history of late payments.

You also want to help people trying to get caught up. Things happen. Life happens—job loss, illness, and so on. We file evictions to get compliance for rent payment, not just to kick people out.

Your threshold for what warrants an eviction is guided by two things: your personal preferences and what is within the law. Make sure you are familiar with laws that govern evictions, including applicable landlord and tenant rights, and have already determined your course of action before you actually need it.

When it's time to file, we usually wait until the fifteenth of the month, but some people file earlier, like the tenth. Regardless, if you let them go longer than twenty days, they never get caught up—but jurisdictions vary, so this should not be construed as legal advice. Consult with your attorney, verify any local laws that govern evictions, and make sure you have covered all your bases before going through the eviction process.

Now there are numerous grounds for an eviction, not just late rental payments. It could be a violation of the lease or an overstay of the lease, for example. Some are going to be easier than others to actually follow through with. Keep in mind, however, that anytime you file an eviction, you need proof of why. For instance, if it is for nonpayment of rent, you will need a lease, a ledger that shows the rent that has not been paid, and a demand letter that will be in compliance with whatever your lease states that you need to do before you can file an eviction. It is so important that you follow all these rules because if you don't, your case could be thrown out and you'll have to start over. Again, I would highly recommend you consult with your local attorney and local laws to make sure you are following this correctly and that your lease is in compliance and following the eviction laws as well.

# Renewals

Most of the time, tenants will want to renew their lease after their current lease expires. That is perfectly okay to do, and this is what I try to do in order to keep everyone in a valid lease. Most of my leases are for a one-year minimum, and of course we perform regular inspections to make sure they are taking care of the property. We also make sure that the rental rates have been increased based on market value to make sure we are in line with what we should be renting the property for.

Now if they do not want to sign a new lease but want to remain for a period of less than one year (or whatever term your current lease requires), then most lease contracts say that it will go into a month-to-month status. They are not required to sign a new lease unless you, as a landlord, prefer that they do so. If your tenant is renting month to month and not currently in a valid lease, then the previous lease is still in place when it comes to the rules that the tenant has to follow. This still allows you to file an eviction for any sort of lease violation, but there are likely provisions in the lease that outline a few new details for when the lease goes month to month. I would highly recommend looking over your lease to make sure, and to verify the way your lease is structured.

# Rental Increases

When leases are up, that is a great time to do rental increases. If a tenant is not in a valid lease, you should provide them a thirty-day written notice of a rental increase. If they are currently in a lease, then you usually would not raise the rent until the lease runs out, and in some jurisdictions, you cannot raise the rent within a lease term. Most of the time, rental leases have provisions in them that allow you to raise rents on someone up to, at a minimum, sixty days before a lease expires, which usually serves as a notice to the tenant that, if they choose to renew, their rent will increase.

If your tenant is currently in a month-to-month status, then most states require a certain amount of time that you have to give notice of a rental increase. This gives you some time to get the information in place and confirm the new rental amounts, and for the tenant to make adjustments to their budget so that everyone is on the same page.

A rental increase cannot be done any time you want or on a whim, especially if you are in a valid lease. Most of these notices need to be in writing so that you have it documented, and I would always follow up with the conversation as well. Rental increases are sometimes very tough conversations with tenants, so you want to make sure that they can absorb the rental increases or that they have time to make other arrangements. There is no point in going up on someone $100 a month if they can only afford $50 a month, because essentially you are forcing an eviction. Think it through—if they are good tenants, pay on time, etc., it may be worth the $50 extra you could charge to hang on to a good tenant instead.

# Landlord and Tenant Rights and Responsibilities

When it comes to landlords' rights and limitations, particularly with applicants, you have to be very careful. You cannot deny somebody's rental application based on discrimination. Denial must be within the letter of the law, and I would highly recommend you consult a local attorney to make sure; otherwise, you are setting yourself up to be sued. It might not be today, but it will be sometime in the near future.

As a landlord, you have a right to protect your property. You have a right to evict a tenant who is tearing up your property, and you also have a right to enter your property if there is imminent danger, if there is an emergency, or if property damage is currently happening. For example, if you are driving by one of your properties and you see water rushing out the front door, you have the right as a landlord to inspect that immediately because that is an emergency.

If you want to perform an inspection or replace the blinds, however, you must give them notice. They cannot deny you access, of course, but you cannot barge in unannounced in these circumstances, either. Your lease should specify what that notice is—usually, twenty-four hours—but your lease must also be compliant with the law. Many times, tenants will tell you that they don't want you to come, or they are not going to let you in; maybe they don't let you in that day, but you can file an eviction on someone who does not allow you to protect your property and to protect your asset, because that is your right as a landlord.

On the flip side, the tenant has rights to privacy within the home that they are renting, so you need to make sure that you are executing your lease accordingly. If you are supposed to give a twenty-four-hour notice before entering, the tenant has the right to deny you access if you don't give a twenty-four-hour notice and show up without warning. So please keep that in mind to keep you out of hot water.

Trust me, you do not want to be on the wrong end of this. It would put you in a terrible position and put your company at risk, which is not something that you want to do—you've worked too hard for that. Do not cut a corner here; paying an attorney for a few hours to make sure you are in compliance with the law will go a long way in protecting your interests.

Most cities have a minimum housing requirement standard that you can access to make sure that your rental adheres to the standards it is supposed to. Laws will vary among jurisdictions, but the majority of the basic information will be the same, meaning the landlord must provide heat, the electrical has to be safe, the plumbing has to be safe, the roof and floors can't have holes, and the home has to be structurally sound, just to name a few.

I highly recommend that you make sure that everything is buttoned up and meets the standards before renting it out, and recheck this at each tenant turnover. When it comes to making some of the repairs, remember, you should have a great process already in place to get them handled. If the repair in question requires a state license to do the work, then you use a state-licensed, certified person to do the work.

Some repairs aren't anticipated, and timeliness can be subjective; when it comes to life safety and minimum housing requirements, I urge you to take care of those immediately. For example, if it is thirty degrees outside and the heat's not working, do not wait a week to call your HVAC repair company—they need to be called immediately. Remember, treat people the way you want to be treated.

I cannot stress enough that it is worth consulting an attorney to ensure you understand your rights as a landlord and their rights as tenants.

# Landlord-Tenant Relationships

While the landlord-tenant relationship is essentially transactional, you still want good relationships with your tenants. That said, there are times when tenant expectations need to be managed.

For example, there are tenants who think every repair is urgent. This is where having a repair-priority system already in place will help you navigate those conversations. A small closet light that's gone out, for example, may be a light bulb that needs to be replaced. Regardless, it is not threatening a life or someone's safety, or not meeting the minimum housing requirements. It is not actively causing damage to your property. Therefore, it is not urgent.

A water leak that only leaks when certain activities take place—flushing a toilet, for example—needs to be addressed expediently, but it is not an emergency. If a gutter falls off the side of a rental house, it needs to be addressed expediently, but it, too, is not an emergency. Have these conversations up front to help set expectations, and if the issue persists, remind them that it is on your radar but that you have a repair-priority system in place for a reason, and you will get to them in time.

This doesn't mean that you neglect your tenants, particularly if there are issues where the property would be deemed uninhabitable—lack of running water, safety issues, backed-up sewer, no heat in the wintertime, and so on. I once had a tenant stop up her toilet and call the city on me because the plumber's schedule was a day out and he could not get there until the next day; the city declared the property uninhabitable because their ordinance said that you had to have operable plumbing. No, I was not the one who stopped up the toilet, but as a landlord, you are responsible for a lot, and the buck always stops with you.

If you have repairs to make due to tenant negligence, you have a decision to make:

- You can make the repairs, allow the tenant to remain in the property, and have the tenant pay you back for the repairs.
- You can file an eviction because the repairs are too great and the tenant would cause too much in additional damages.
- You can file an eviction because the repairs are too great and proceed with necessary repairs for anything that is a life-safety issue.
- You can see if the tenant will leave voluntarily and sign an agreement or payment plan to compensate for repairs, or take legal action to require that they do so.

Regardless, I would recommend handling all of these on a case-by-case basis because if it is a life-safety item and it makes the property uninhabitable, then it would make sense to have a sense of urgency and get it taken care of in a timely manner. If the house just needs some repairs, normally we go ahead and fix what needs to be fixed and bill the tenant later, or file an eviction on the tenant for the damages they have done.

Now if a property becomes uninhabitable because of tenant neglect, I will file an eviction immediately to make sure it is on record. Why? The tenant might try to come after you because they are currently staying in an uninhabitable house. I know they shouldn't be staying in an uninhabitable house, but sometimes tenants don't want to leave, so they will put the blame on the landlord.

If there is any sort of imminent danger within the house that made it uninhabitable—a gas leak, for example—while you are waiting on the eviction process, I would see if an agreement could be reached between you and your tenant to get them out of the unsafe house. There again, you want to try to do the right thing and always protect yourself in case something happens while the process is ongoing.

Now there is a difference between normal wear and tear and actual damages. Normal wear and tear would be the wearing of carpet where someone has repeatedly walked, for example; after five years or so, that carpet isn't going to look brand-new. Whereas if you have holes in your wall, that would be considered damage.

Wear and tear cannot be deducted from a deposit, but damages can be deducted. Make sure that you have everything documented correctly when you are looking at normal wear and tear versus damages, including photos of anything that you have deducted out of a deposit, so that their deposit can be refunded correctly.

There needs to be a detailed abandonment clause in your lease. Abandonment occurs when the property is rented and your tenant leaves the property beyond a specified amount of time (i.e., they didn't just go on vacation). Sometimes, they do this to skip out on rent, but regardless, you never hear from them again. I've had this happen several times throughout my career as a landlord; usually they just stop paying rent, we send them notices, and we do not hear back from them. When we go to the property, they are gone, usually taking most of their belongings with them. Again, make sure there are provisions within the lease on how to handle abandonment, and proceed accordingly if it happens to you.

When situations get sticky—tenants are denying you entry, for example, or they claim they didn't do the damage and therefore refuse to pay for the repair, or outright abandon the property—if your attorney has reviewed your lease to make sure it follows the law, then you can reference your lease if the conversation gets heated. Your lease should outline quite plainly what each party's responsibilities are, and you have that in writing, on a document that you both signed. And if necessary, a document that should be strong enough to stand up in a court of law.

# Stick to the Basics and Stay Open to Change

Earlier in the chapter, I mentioned that the rental process is complex. When you think about the layers of responsibility—execution, following the law, having proper procedures in place, handling repairs—there are a number of rabbit holes you can fall into easily. But in reality, the rental process can also be very simple if you stick to the basics and stay open to change. Things are always evolving. Stay educated on trends, markets, and laws. Stay open to new ideas and new ways of doing things, like your application process. Stay open to change...trust me, that is exactly where I am right now, and you never know where life will take you.

I still remember talking to a Realtor and talking to several friends that suggested I could really help people learn this business. A lot of people would love to know what's in my head and to be able to replicate my success. In the next chapter, we'll discuss when enough is enough, and what that means to me—and possibly, to you.

# Chapter 13
# When Is Enough "Enough"?

During the height of the pandemic, I started to think about when enough is actually *enough*. I think a lot of people can relate to this, maybe in a few different ways.

For me, the world was in a tough position at that time, and it got me thinking about why we are really on this earth. I have a lot of drive and pursued the dreams that I had for myself, setting very high expectations. High expectations are not bad; in fact, my parents always taught me to have high expectations for myself. But the real question for me was "Do I spend my whole life going after my own dreams?" After spending all my good years doing that, would I arrive at the end of my life and have only a few years left to enjoy what took my entire life to accomplish?

Boy, was that a loaded question for me!

Many lives were ruined because of the pandemic, and the restrictions left many of us in a place where comfort was measured and masked. Hugs and even someone's presence had to be restricted. So many people had spent their entire lives working hard to provide for their families, hoping to leave a legacy in the end, only to have the pandemic rip it away—lives and livelihoods lost.

At the end of the day, do you really want to spend your entire life accumulating a bunch of different assets and items just to leave them to someone else, and you yourself will not be around to enjoy any of it? Shouldn't our focus be on what makes us happy and less about what we might leave someone?

When is enough actually...*enough*?

Perhaps enough is a combination of realizing your dreams but also realizing what's actually most important in life. Up to the point of the COVID-19 pandemic, my goals and priorities were big dreams for myself and my family—getting into real estate and growing a scalable real estate company that I would be proud of. When I was a young boy, that drive to be the best possible person I could be was instilled in me and has only grown—and I learned even more about healthy competition and teamwork through playing sports. By 2020, I had hundreds of units and was still buying; I started new ventures, which brought new revenue streams. I did not, however, have the best work–life balance, because there again, the world tells you to just work, work, work to obtain your goals and dreams instead of really living.

Why was I working myself into an early grave just to leave something to someone else when I die? Sure, it's a morbid thing to think about, but I think it is a valid question to ask yourself. It shifted my mindset to something like *Yes, I have goals and I have dreams, and I have realized those, but what would my twenty-five-year-old self think about what I have accomplished?*

# Bigger Isn't Always Better

A wise woman once told me that "bigger isn't always better," and I did not fully understand that until I had something that was bigger. The world will tell you that you should go bigger and do more, but that isn't always the right answer. You can create a business that's super big and super successful, where you make millions a year and have way more than you've ever dreamed of having. But if you're not enjoying the journey, none of that matters.

As you accumulate things, your mindset will change. Owning five or ten rental units may seem like a lot to most people, until you meet someone who owns two hundred. That person's perspective is likely going to be a little different. Take a moment to assess; if you are not enjoying the journey, then take another moment to reassess. Bigger isn't always better if your joy is eroding in the process.

I well remember asking myself:

- Why put yourself through misery?
- If you are not going to enjoy it, why create a rental property company that has hundreds of units?
- If you're not going to enjoy it, if you don't have a good work–life balance, and if you don't have enough time to spend with family and friends, then why are you doing this at all?

All of this was going through my mind during the pandemic, and it helped me reassess what actually mattered in my life.

# What Is "Enough"?

When you think about what it means to have enough, and how that evolves over time, you really should backtrack to what your original goals and dreams were. If you had told me when I was fifteen or twenty years old that I would own several hundred rental units, flip houses, lend money, launch a consulting business, and write a book by age thirty-five, I would have told you that was crazy and that there was no way I would have attained all that!

My dreams weren't very big back then, but they did evolve over time. You can be way more successful than you could ever imagine if you have the right base, get it right the first time, and put one foot in front of the other to do what is required of you on a daily basis.

As you proceed, the question is inevitable: *Do I have enough?*

You can't determine whether you have enough if you don't have something to compare it to—your younger self—realizing that you have exceeded the dreams you had for yourself. That does evolve over time, however, and it's not something that you realize you have done just in the moment; you have to look back to see what your dreams used to be, and if your dreams are much bigger than what they used to be, then you are probably headed down the right road. But I would also advise not to focus solely on your own dreams...and maybe see how you could assist someone else's.

When you start thinking about whether you have enough, think about what your twenty-five-year-old self might think if they could see into the future and look at what they will accomplish. Think about where your head was at that age, what success meant to you in comparison to what it means to you now. This will give you some clarity for what you might want out of life, and it will certainly give you a great gauge of whether what you have is enough. If you stay in accumulation mode and don't take time to consider whether it's enough or too much, you miss the blessings of what you have currently.

# Have a Vision, a Plan, and Goals

Yes, I had dreams at age twenty-five, but if I didn't have a vision, plan, or goals in place, then I would not have achieved them. Each day, there is something you can do to work toward your dreams. You set goals to keep you on track; otherwise, when things don't happen overnight, it's too easy to abandon your plans. Whether your goals are monthly, quarterly, annual, or all of the above, they can keep you accountable on those days when you are tired and want to give up.

Goals are measurable and allow you to track your progress. Otherwise, you have no way to assess your progress to see if you're headed in the right direction.

If you want to attain something, you have to create a clear vision of what you want and a good plan with measurable results. It doesn't have to be an elaborate plan, just a plan that can get you there.

# Living versus Accumulating

How do you know whether your business is allowing you to live more, or just accumulate more? Don't confuse the two. My eyes were opened to this during the pandemic; I was raised with a solid foundation about what's truly important in life and have tried to live out the values I was raised with. I thought I had a firm grasp of this, and the pandemic forced me to go deeper, look longer, and think harder. It was eye-opening.

It is perfectly okay to have dreams and goals to have a nice house, a vacation home, and a car, or take fancy vacations, accumulate wealth, and so on, but that shouldn't be your sole focus. Those things are fun, but that's not really living—that's accumulating.

Living is much more than just accumulating. It's quieter, less obvious, and much, much richer. Pre-pandemic, I focused squarely on continuing to grow my rental property company, which was already a couple hundred units strong, and I wanted to purchase even more units. If I was already a multimillionaire, why did I need to accumulate more assets and more income? For what purpose?

I already had seven figures coming in, already in the top 1 percent net worth in the country, so why did I really need anything more? I don't want to be a seventy-year-old CEO of a company and realize that I have waited and worked my entire life to reach the top, only to have a few years to actually enjoy the fruits of my labor. That would be a very sad place to arrive.

If you ask the majority of CEOs of companies, I would wager that they would tell you they wished they would have enjoyed life a little bit more. They probably wish they had gone to their sons' or daughters' sporting events, band concerts, or birthday parties instead of working or traveling for work when those were taking place. You can't get those moments back, after all.

There is a huge movement in this country where people are realizing that they are working their entire lives to accumulate wealth, but it will take them an entire lifetime to get there. This movement asks the same questions I was asking myself: What's the point? What's the purpose? Why am I solely focused on accumulating and acquiring, in order to leave those assets for someone else to enjoy?

In the same spirit, I would challenge you to live before it's too late. I promise that you do not want to miss out on those parts of life that truly matter, because once you miss them, they are gone forever. If the job that you have doesn't allow you to take in these events with your family and friends, then maybe you should evaluate whether or not you have the right job.

Look, sometimes we have to miss things. If you have bills and need the overtime, I understand that you're between a rock and a hard place. But if you constantly miss these moments, then maybe you should evaluate what you're doing. I know that's what I did before I got into the rental business. I was working as a retail store manager, working twelve hours a day, and missing out on things I wanted to do. I took a leap of faith and got into the rental business, and eventually, it became my full-time career.

It has been a life changer; now, I try not to miss anything. When one of my best friends is having a son, I get on a plane to Nashville, Tennessee, to be there for the blessed event. When one of my best friends is getting married in Alabama, I hop on a plane and go. When another friend decides to run for political office, and he needs help, I get on a plane and go help. When my parents and brother want to get away and go to the beach and have a fun family weekend, I get in the car and go to the beach. I want to live before it's too late because nobody is guaranteed tomorrow. Don't take those life events and loved ones for granted.

And for someone who still works those long hours and is trying to get into real estate, it's going to be hard—but I am living proof that it's doable. You will have days that you struggle, but while you "plan out your plan" to become successful in real estate, you can start "working to live" by just showing up—whether that means getting off work early to go to your son's or daughter's soccer game, going to a family birthday party, going to a game night at a friend's house, or just taking a day off to spend time with your family. It doesn't have to be extravagant. Just showing up means you are taking the first steps to live more.

Now, I no longer live to work, but I work to live. If you live to work, that means you are getting up on a daily basis for the sole purpose on this earth of accumulating assets. But when you have that mindset of working to live, yes, you still work, but now you are focusing on living life and using the fruits of your labor, your hard-earned money, to actually live life and enjoy life. Life is short, after all. I was thirty-four when I realized this, and I wish I would have realized this earlier. Now, a lot of my decisions are based on working to live, and not living to work. When you have that mindset, then your perspective on life changes a lot.

Maybe you already love the job you're in. I love my work, too. There is nothing wrong with that, but I do think you need to put boundaries and safeguards in place to make sure that's not all you're doing, Honestly, I could do the rental business 24/7, but I needed to put boundaries in place because I was missing out on other things in life that truly mattered. I didn't want to wake up fifty years down the road and have regrets. Put safeguards in place that still allow you to do what you love to do and stay passionate about what you do but also enjoy the other things that life offers that don't have anything to do with work.

# Don't Miss the Journey

I always tell people that you should enjoy the journey. In fact, the reason my latest venture, SOARX, is styled in all capital letters is because clients will be coached on their initial dreams and destinations, but more importantly, they will be coached every step of the way—all the stuff that happens in between the dream and destination—so that they enjoy the journey.

After all, the destination is a moving target, and as a result, most of us never fully obtain it. For instance, if someone has a dream of owning ten rental properties, and they reach that dream, now they want twenty, and eventually, they'll want fifty, and so on. That was me. I just wanted ten units so that I could have some secondary income. I could have stopped there, but I wanted to keep going, keep going, and keep going. That destination was a moving target.

Remember the advice Joel gave me early on? Slow down. Enjoy the journey. Don't miss the blessings that are happening along the way. Otherwise, you will miss out on a lot of life lessons, too. You never know when your last day on this earth will be, so don't spend your whole life just looking at the destination and missing out on what matters.

Many people think that money is going to solve all their problems and fix everything for them. There is a tipping point that comes with financial stability and independence versus a money grab. Money can also bring about problems that you would not encounter otherwise. I know what it is to be that guy making $40,000–$50,000 a year and being $75,000 in debt. In many respects, money may have been even more attractive to me in those days, but there is a point where you shift from being independent and financially stable to just grabbing what you can get.

Some peace comes with financial stability and independence, but just having those two things will not bring you real peace. During the pandemic,

I was making seven figures a year. I was financially stable, I was independent, and I did not have the peace I was looking for. I had been focusing on the wrong thing; I was living to work instead of working to live. Way too many people out there say that money brings happiness; I can promise you that it will not, and I am speaking from experience. If you do not care about your mental well-being and having peace in life, it won't matter how much money you have, because your mental health will suffer.

Yes, having financial stability and independence helps, but if you do not take care of your mental health and spend time with the people who matter most, you will be living a lonely life. A lonely life is not a good life.

It doesn't mean that you have to see everyone every day of the week; rather, you want to live a full life, one that is not all business, not about meeting and exceeding a certain income level, not just about attaining a particular net worth, but having genuine relationships and friendships with friends and family. Because at the end of the day, that's the missing piece that brings you peace. When you have good relationships with others, when you are doing the right things on a daily basis, when you have a great relationship with God...those will get you through life's battles. Because whether you have money or not, you will still face battles from time to time.

Sickness, depression, and tragedy don't care if you're financially stable or not. They will arrive, regardless. Make sure you have more in life than just a successful business.

# The Other Thing You Accumulate

Here is something else you will accumulate if your focus remains strictly on accumulation: stress.

Yes, I am financially independent. I have a high net worth. I have a good income stream, with backup income streams. I am also more stressed today than when I was in my early twenties with $75,000 of student loan debt and no rental properties. Let that sink in.

Sure, I had stress in my early twenties, but it was stress about different things: *How am I going to attain my dreams and goals? How am I going to pay off my student loans? How am I going to have enough money to make ends meet this month?*

Today, my stress is different. The more properties you own, the more expenses you will have. You'll have taxes, insurance, maintenance, and mortgages...for hundreds of properties. You are employing people to help you manage that, and you need to pay them fairly, which I take very seriously. Now, my stress has a direct impact on others' livelihoods. It is no longer about how I am going to make ends meet—it's about how they are going to make ends meet and how they will thrive, and knowing that largely rests on my shoulders.

I have created a company that I am proud of, and I employ good people to help me, but now I have to make sure I am doing not only what is best for the company but also doing what is best for them. They have put their trust in me, and I am committed to doing a great job for them. That is a huge stressor for me; if my company were to go out of business, then it would not only affect my life, but now it would also affect the lives of my employees and their families. That can keep you up at night if you are not handling things correctly.

# Who Decides?

Finally, who decides when enough is *enough*?

Put your phone down and get off social media. Don't think about what the world says you should have, or shouldn't have. Don't look to your right or left to see what others have, or think about how you'll compare to others at your next high school reunion. You shouldn't compare yourself to anyone else because you are you, and no one else. Do not give someone else the power to answer that question for you. You don't know what the next person is going through to get (or cling to) what they have; they may be facing struggles similar to yours, or worse. Only you can determine when enough is enough. Look back at your younger self; if you could have a conversation with them, would they be proud? Only you can answer that. Make sure you are not allowing others to influence what that might be. This is not a popularity contest. It is a contest between your ears—inside your own mind. Not anyone else's.

I go back to the advice Joel gave me: slow down. Take a moment to think about your definition of *enough*.

If it costs you a great real estate deal, so be it. I promise you another one will come along. It's not the end. Not by a longshot. Maybe there was a reason that deal happened while you were over there thinking about what matters in your life—and maybe, just maybe, you sidestepped a landmine in the process.

I believe that we are on this earth for much more than just what a job or a rental property company can give us. I believe we are on this earth because there is a higher priority called God. A lot of the decisions I make in business reflect my values, and if it doesn't align with my faith in God, I don't do it. Make sure that your decisions align with your values and who you want to become.

The great thing about this is you get to decide what those values are. There is no right or wrong answer; just determine who you want to be and how you will live your life in order to be that person. For me, faith is important; throughout my life and throughout the success I have had in real estate, I've kept God close. I pray daily to ask God for guidance. When I "miss out" on what appeared to be a good deal, it's not unusual for me to discover down the road that there were problems with a property that were not apparent at the time. My faith leads me in the right direction, and the direction that God wants me to go.

No, God did not just drop a successful real estate company in my lap. I didn't "name it and claim it," so to speak. There were things I had to do, and continue to do, on a daily basis to get me there. I am proud of what I have accomplished, but I am even prouder to say I've done it with God walking hand in hand with me.

So finally, I will ask one more time: when is enough...*enough*?

Only you can answer that question for yourself. No one else can answer it for you, nor can you answer that for someone else's situation. We all tend to play the comparison game every now and then, but it's pointless. It's a waste of time.

I have given you a lot of things to think about to help you determine your own threshold of enough. Everyone has their own journey and therefore, their own story...and their own definition of *enough*. This is about what you want in life and what will give you peace and enjoyment in life.

Your gut, peace, and your faith should be your guide. In a way, you serve as your own North Star.

I have enough. Now, I'm looking at the next chapter in my life—to be able to help others realize their dreams. SOARX Consulting is dedicated to helping average Americans on a path to a successful rental property business. Through coaching and coursework, clients receive a step-by-step process on how to realize their own dreams of real estate investing.

Please feel free to reach out. You are your own North Star, but I am here to help you blaze your trail.

# Conclusion

Everyday people can get into real estate without having any great wealth or powerful connections; you now have a blueprint to get started. I am still an everyday American; the only difference between you and me is that I've been working at it for several years now. This book has provided you with the foundation that you need to get started; these were the exact steps that I took to create a successful rental property business.

Without these steps, you are stacking the odds against yourself. Just owning rental property is not enough; the rental properties need to produce income and a net profit for you. You do not want to own a property for years and not make a profit.

## A Recap of Items to Remember

Here are a few items to take with you while you work on your next steps.

1. Your lender needs you as much as you need them. The person who finances the property has a job to do, and that job is to loan you money. That's what they get paid to do, but their job is to be selective in the process—loan money to good people who are responsible and would make a good client for the bank. So on the flip side, you also need financial backing. You need the lender to help you by financing that first purchase—that will launch your real estate business.

2. There is a fine line between saving money and cutting corners. You don't have to pay top dollar for rental properties or pay top dollar for maintaining them, but you never want to cut a corner either. Do your due diligence on purchases, and get all maintenance and repair terms in writing. You are responsible for getting things done right. Do the work up front and get it right the first time, or it costs you time and money down the road.

3. The money you make or save does not need to be spent on cars, boats, or other depreciating assets. You want to use your hard-earned money for things that are going to make you money down the road. If you have systems in place before you need them, this will be much easier to manage. Make sure that you have a good rental management process in place, whether or not you use software to do it. You need a good filing system so that you know where all your important documents are and that they are stored safely. When you need them, you don't have time to search for them; you just need to know where they are. Remember to have a good maintenance system in place, where you have great vendors you can rely on when things go wrong. If you do it correctly, it will also save you thousands of dollars.

4. Never say never. You need to do what it takes to prepare for the unthinkable and the things that "would never happen." None of us can predict the future, but there are plenty of things we can do to protect ourselves, our assets, our businesses, and our tenants. Insurance companies will not advocate for you, so you need to advocate for yourself by including extra protections, like trusts and LLCs. You have to be your biggest advocate.

5. Always remember to do the right thing, even if it's not popular. You want to be a good person, have good morals and values, and do the right thing—always. Remember the example I gave you earlier in the book, the house that was rented by the room? I had to make the unpopular decision to push back because that was the right thing to do for the people who lived at that property. Sometimes, doing the right thing will not be easy—in fact, the stress of it may keep you up at night—but in the end, you need to do it. If you don't have morals and values, then what do you have at all? You will never know everything there is to know about this business, so seek and surround yourself with those who have been there before you; they are the ones who have true wisdom and can help guide you through those difficult, unpopular-but-right decisions.

6. My parents always told me never to put all my eggs in one basket. This applies to your real estate business too. As you continue to expand your rental business and buy rental properties, maybe you start to look at flipping houses as an alternative income to help support your rental business and provide short-term income. Or

perhaps there are some high-interest accounts you can put some money into that provide some interest income. As you continue to expand and become more seasoned, maybe you start thinking about lending money; now, you're making money on top of the money that you have lent, and you are making interest income every month.

7. The rental property business and process is very simple, so long as you stick to the basics and stay open to change, because things evolve. Remember, I used to do things the old-fashioned way; I would meet prospective tenants in person and have them complete an application or lease, but now I have rental management software that allows me to ask the same questions and secure the same application or lease—and now no one has to take time off from work or time away from other things to get the same work done. When you stay open to learning, you never know what avenues may open up that will help you find a better path, new ventures, and new relationships.

8. Finally, never compare yourself to others. Only you can answer the question of when enough is *enough*. It's not anyone else's responsibility to answer that for you. Yes, you are going to make money, but this is more about where your heart is. I know it's a vulnerable conversation with the brain between your ears, but it will pay dividends down the road if you can answer it.

# SOARX

For me personally, I have arrived at the "enough" part in the rental business. I am so blessed to have what I have today, and now I am ready to help others. I have reached the point where instead of continuing to grow my rental business, I want to maintain it and turn my focus toward helping others through my consulting business called SOARX Consulting. In my spare time, I earned my pilot's license and enjoy flying planes. When you fly, you are soaring upward until you hit the desired altitude. And if $X$ marks the spot, then $X$ is the goal you're flying toward, and you're soaring upward until you reach it. If the destination is all that you focus on, you will miss a lot of blessings throughout life. The blessings far outweigh the heartaches. This is how I came up with the name, SOARX, in all caps, because it's not just about the destination, but it's about the entire journey.

SOARX Consulting was launched because I want to help everyday Americans, just like myself, succeed in the real estate business. I offer coaching services and have created an online course that takes you through a step-by-step process on a more in-depth level to get you there. This is the exact step-by-step process that I have used over the last decade, and I want you to be just as successful as I have been. I did this because I do not want the next generation of landlords to never actually become landlords, thinking they lack the money or connections to get them there.

Having coaches and mentors in this business pays dividends far beyond what you can measure. If I can help you in this way, please reach out to me via my website, www.SOARXconsulting.com, and let's continue the conversation we have started. I have all the faith in the world that you are going to do amazing things, but first you have to do something uncomfortable—take the first step. I was right where you were just a few years ago, and I'm so glad I stepped out of my comfort zone to take the leap of faith.

Now it's your turn.

# Acknowledgments

I want to thank the following people who have inspired me in my life, business, and writing this book: my mom and dad, my brother, my great-granny, my grandparents, my aunt, other special family members, my extended family, my best friends, my extended friends, my mentors, my bankers, my lawyers, my Realtors, my vendors and team members, teachers, coaches, book coach, publisher, my real estate professor, and other professors and faculty at High Point University.

I want to thank EVERYONE who has ever helped me before and during my time in the rental business. You all played a big part in my success.

I want to thank God most of all, because without God, I wouldn't be able to do any of this.

# About the Author

Remembering how hard it was to overcome his own doubts and insecurities in the beginning of his investment career, Steven Andrews is now on a mission to empower others to achieve their own goals in real estate. In addition to writing, *The New American Dream: A Simple Roadmap to Purchasing Investment Properties,* Steven established SOARX Consulting, where he provides an eleven-week course outlining the same process he used to create his rental property company. The program, like the book, offers a roadmap to finding the kind of success Steven has in the business called real estate.

To connect with Steven directly, you can email him at coach@soarxconsulting.com.

You can learn more about his course from his website: SOARXConsulting.com.

And you can find him online:

- Facebook at SOARX Consulting

- Instagram: @soarx_consulting

- Linkedin: Steven Andrews

- YouTube: @soarxconsulting

Milton Keynes UK
Ingram Content Group UK Ltd.
UKHW021044160324
439394UK00006B/151/J